The Irish in Dakota

by
David Kemp

Mariah Press
2nd Printing
1995

The Irish in Dakota

Published by
Mariah Press
Sioux Falls, SD 57105

ISBN 0-9624593-1-3
Library of Congress Catalog Number 92-90983

FIRST EDITION
2nd Printing, Revised with Index

Edited and designed by Randy Califf
Cover design and photography by Randy Califf

Printed by Pine Hill Press, Inc., Freeman, South Dakota
Manufactured in the United States of America

ACKNOWLEDGEMENTS

I would like to thank my parents, Warren and Margaret Aylward Kemp, for providing me with the perspective which I developed in this account. Yes, I am more Irish than my father.

Thanks to my grandmother, Charlotte Beck Kemp, who told me stories of the United Irishmen and the Uprising of 1798 that she heard from her grandmother, Mary McGivern McDermott. She has kept these stories in her memory in spite of several attempts to keep her from remembering anything.

Thanks to Marian Devitt, who always talks of the experiences of early Dakota in the same way that she taught them, with respect, validity, and exceptional humor. I hope that I will continue on the spiritual traditions of Irish history tellers that I have inherited.

Thanks to Father James Joyce and Bishop Paul Dudley for the opportunity to experience the accounts found in the Catholic Diocese of Sioux Falls Archives. Thanks to the Diocese in Rapid City for a similar experience.

Thanks to Herbert Hoover and Michael Funchion for the challenge to bring the Irish experience to a proper historical stature. This account will not threaten the strength of enduring oral traditions of the region. I hope that this account inspires similar excursions into our most interesting past.

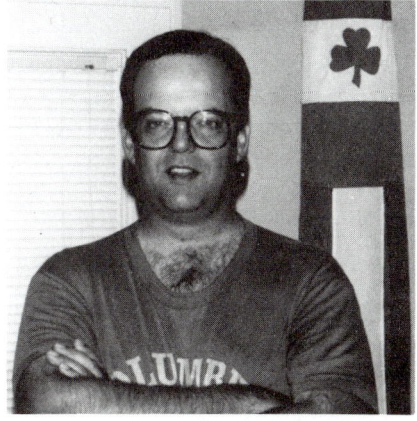

Author David Kemp

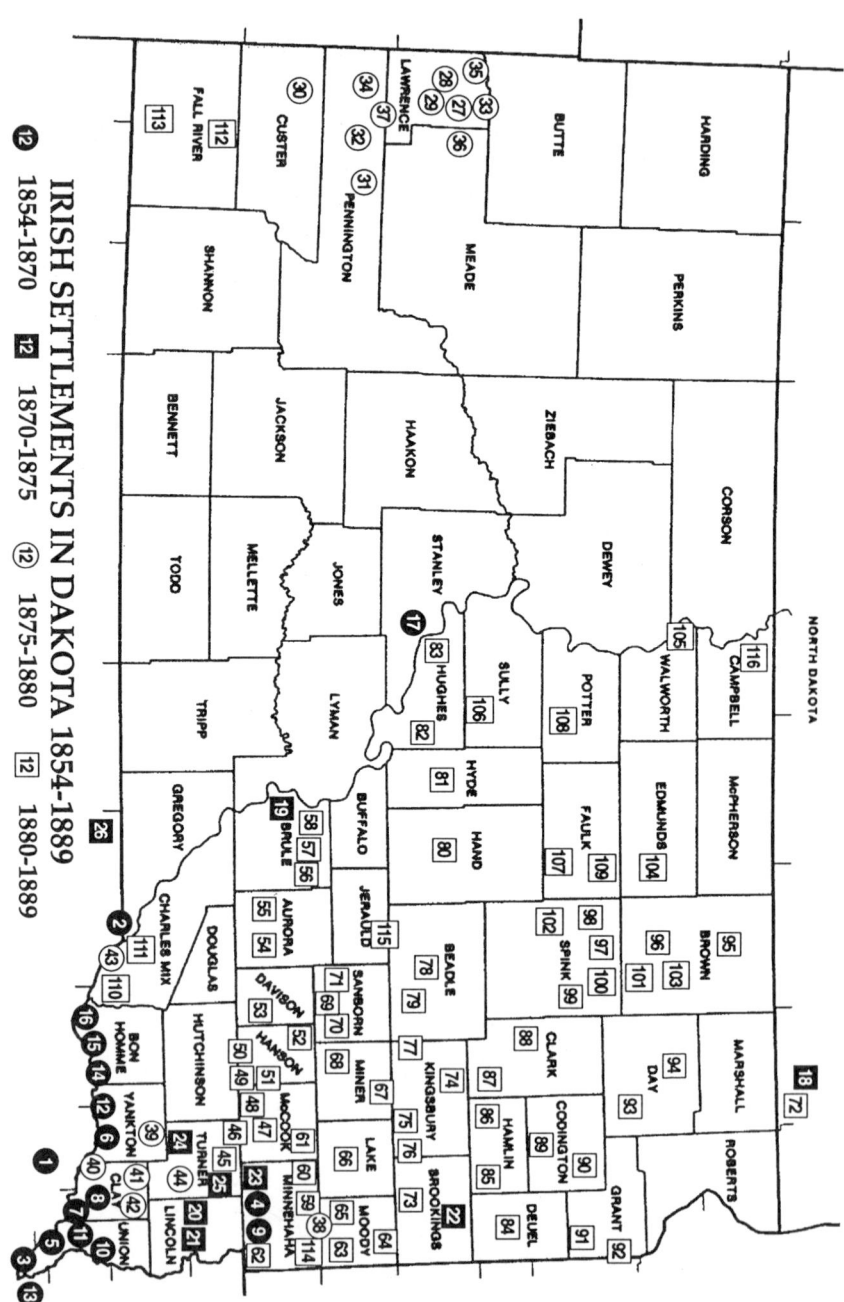

IRISH SETTLEMENTS IN DAKOTA 1854-1889

⑫ 1854-1870   🄵 1870-1875   ⑫ 1875-1880   🄵 1880-1889

IRISH SETTLEMENTS, DAKOTA TERRITORY AND SURROUNDING REGION 1854-1889

Settlements shown on the map on page iv are cross-referenced in the book text with brackets [xx] at the end of the related sentence.

1854 - 1870
1) St. John's City, Jackson, Nebraska
2) Fort Randall
3) Chris Mahoney's Post
4) Western Land Company, Falls of Sioux River
5) Twelve Mile House, Big Sioux Point, Jefferson
6) John Stanage's Post
7) Fort Vermillion, James McHenry's Post
8) Bloomingdale
9) Fort Dakota
10) Emmett
11) Garryowen
12) Yankton
13) Sioux City
14) Bon Homme
15) Springfield
16) Running Water
17) Fort Pierre

1870-75
18) St. Joseph, Pembina Mountain
19) Brule City
20) Lennox
21) Worthing

22) Elkton
23) Celton, West Minnehaha County
24) Swan Lake
25) Finley
26) O'Neill, Nebraska

1875 - 1880
27) Deadwood
28) Central City
29) Lead
30) Custer
31) Rapid City
32) Silver City
33) Crook City, Whitewood
34) Galena
35) Spearfish
36) Fort Meade, Sturgis
37) Rockerville
38) St. Michael's, Moody County
39) Walshtown
40) Wakonda
41) Lodi
42) Star Corners
43) Wheeler
44) Turner

TABLE OF CONTENTS

INTRODUCTION

This narrative of the experiences of Irish people in Territorial Dakota is an exceptional account of the Irish American experience in 19th Century America. The Irish who came to Dakota were inspired to leave the crowded cities of the east in order to find a more secure and religious existence. Many came to Dakota to find a land similar to the land they had left. Ireland was a rural and remote land of extreme beauty. For centuries the people of Ireland had centered their lives around rural communities. Communities based on farming and a strong relationship to their clan. The men raised livestock and grain crops. The women raised large families and operated the family and the farm from the kitchen of the families' dwellings. Towns consisted of nothing more than a few buildings and the parish church. The church was the center of the community's activity. Driven by the English occupation and the Great Famine, Irish people were forced to leave their homeland into eternal exile. They had been forced by poverty into the squalor of the industrial cities of the American East. What remained of the spirituality of the Irish people in America was to be preserved, and perhaps replanted by moving to the American West.

In 1881 James Spalding, the Roman Catholic Bishop of Peoria, Illinois, published the book, <u>The Religious Mission of the Irish People and Catholic Colonization</u>. In his series of essays Bishop Spalding used his position as one of America's leading Catholic clergy to create official, church sanction for the concept of American Catholic colonization in the West. What the concept meant was " the systematic and deliberate effort to take people from the great cities and factory towns, from the mines and railroads, from domestic service in hotels and private houses, and to place them upon the cheap and fertile land of our country".[1]

A major contribution of the Irish people in the many centuries of Christianity was the preservation of Christian beliefs by Irish Celtic monks. These scholarly individuals, isolated in monasteries on the Island of Ireland, preserved the concepts and religious perspectives of early Christianity during the centuries in which the Roman Empire collapsed and Europe was ravaged by various, "barbaric" invaders. A century ago in America the Irish people, in Spalding's eyes, the spiritual descendants of the Celtic monks, lived in the crowded slums of the cities of the Eastern United States. Many had been born soon after their families had fled to America due to the Great Famine in Ireland.

James Spalding was a rare breed, a descendent of English Catholics who arrived in Maryland in the 1690's. Spalding found a religious bond with the Irish American Catholics. He believed that it was the religious mission of himself and the Irish people,because of his and their unique religious experience, to lead American Catholics in a colonization movement to preserve the true spirituality of Roman Catholicism.

The Irish Americans needed to escape the poverty and sinful vices of the crowded slums. Small communities were to be created in which the center of activities was to be the church. The family unit was to be preserved by returning to the land as farmers. Returning to the land as farmers who could receive the benefits of their toil. An experience denied them in Ireland after the English seizure of the land in the 17th and 18th centuries. The Irish served as peasants on their ancestral homelands. They were forced to eat only potatoes. The animals and grains that they worked to produce were taken by the English landlords and shipped outside of the country. Spalding believed that only in this return to the land was the positive spiritual nature of Roman Catholicism existing in America to be preserved.

In conjunction with Archbishop Ireland of St. Paul and Bishop James O'Connor of Omaha, Spalding encouraged Catholic Colonization in the Upper Midwest. These officially sanctioned efforts in the late 1870s by prominent Roman Catholic clergy led official credence to beliefs held and efforts made by many Irish Americans as early as the late 1840s. These experiences are presented in this account.

Organized colonization efforts by Irish people to settle in the region began as early as 1854. Soon after the opening of Nebraska

Territory in 1854 a group of Irish settlers, led by Father Jerimiah Trecy, came from Dubuque, Iowa and established a colony called St. John's City. The settlement was located on the bluffs of the Missouri River, eight miles west of present day Sioux City, Iowa.[2] [1]

Formal colonization efforts began with Archbishop John Ireland of St. Paul, Minnesota, through the Irish Emigration Society, which eventually became the Catholic Colonization Bureau. These efforts created several Catholic communities throughout Minnesota and influenced Irish settlement in Dakota.

Bishop James O'Connor, through the Catholic Colonization Bureau in Omaha participated in the establishment of settlements throughout Nebraska. The most notable were the Greeley and O'Neill settlements.[26] Correspondence between Bishop O'Connor and his missionary for Dakota Territory, Martin Marty, indicates the intention of establishing a similar Catholic colony in Dakota Territory.[3] Bishop James O'Connor was responsible for inviting the Presentation Sisters, an order of Irish Catholic Sisters, to locate in Dakota Territory.[4] The Presentation Order provided teachers that were to teach the children of Native Americans and Catholic immigrants to the area.

In 1880 Martin Marty, recently appointed Bishop of the Vicariate of Dakota, and Father Christian Knauf, pastor and land agent of St. Adrian, a Catholic Colonization Bureau colony in Southwestern Minnesota, together purchased land on the bluffs overlooking the settlement of Sioux Falls.[5] [4] St. Michael's Church was built on the property. The present St. Joseph's Cathedral is located on the site. In 1879, Father William Maher, the first resident pastor of St. Michael's, was ordained in Milwaukee by Bishop Spalding. He was sent immediately to the Sioux Falls community.

Many Irish Americans migrated from the formally established colonies in Minnesota and Nebraska to less formally organized settlements in Dakota Territory. All of these colonization efforts were in response to the call of the Bishops to return to small, rural, religious, oriented communities on the land.

As this study was carried out the author knew of many people, like himself, who are descendants of these people who responded to the call to move West. It is easy to understand why my McDermott ancestors sold their dairy and coal mine outside of Peoria, Illinois and migrated to Northwestern Iowa, forty miles east of Sioux Falls in 1881. Why the Maddens and the Devitts moved to the Worthing area in the 1870s. Many of the people of the region have found similar experiences in their family's past. All part of what Spalding, O'Connor, and Ireland believed was our religious mission.

This study documents the events and experiences, beginning with the St. John's City settlement in 1854 and ending with South Dakota statehood in 1889. I hope to possibly shed some insight to the beliefs and intentions of the Irish people who settled in the region in the 19th Century. This study will be limited to the Irish American experience in Dakota Territory.from 1854 through 1889. An expanded study must include an examination of Irish settlement in the whole upper midwest area. A latter study must also include Irish American settlement in West River South Dakota after the opening of the Great Sioux Reservation in 1889.

1   The Religious Mission of the Irish People and Catholic Colonization, by J.L. Spalding,(The Catholic Publication Society Company, 1881, New York), Pages 141-142.

2   History of the Catholic Church in Nebraska, by Henry Casper, S.J.,(Bruce Press,Milwaukee, 1960), Pages 66-95.

3   Letter: Martin Marty to James O'Connor, June 30, 1880; Archdiocese of Omaha Archives.

4   Letters: Mother DeSales Carrick to James O'Connor and Martin Marty, November 29,30, 1877; Archdiocese of Omaha Archives. This correspondence answers the question: In 1879 Martin Marty was consecrated in Rome as the Bishop of the Vicariate of Dakota. How did Martin Marty know on his way back to the United States that he was suppose to stop in Ireland to pick up the Presentation Sisters? They had been waiting for over two years to come over. A comprehensive history of the Presentation Sisters is found in Women With Vision, The Presentation Sisters of South Dakota, 1880-1985 by Susan Peterson and Courtney Vaughn-Roberson, University of Illinois Press, Urbana, 1988.

5   Deed Record "H", County of Minnehaha, Territory of Dakota, September 30, 1880.

CHAPTER 1

INITIAL SETTLEMENT IN THE REGION

Sometime in 1854, Mathias Loras, the Irish born Bishop of Dubuque, whose Catholic Church jurisdiction included present-day Nebraska and South Dakota, developed the idea of starting a colony of Irish settlers in the newly created Nebraska Territory. The Kansas-Nebraska Act was enacted on May 29, 1854. In 1855, a group of sixty settlers, described as all Irish but a handful of German Catholics, and led by Jerimiah Trecy, an Irish born Catholic priest, moved across the Missouri River at the site of present-day Sioux City, Iowa into Nebraska Territory. They established a settlement called St. John's City. [1] It was to be part of St. Patrick's colony and was situated on the Missouri River bluffs near a flowing spring. The location was approximately ten miles west of the community engaged in the organization of Sioux City. Settlers in the first group, which arrived at the location in June of 1855, included Michael and Patrick Ryan, and James McHenry.[1]

In 1855, the U.S. Army established a post along the Missouri River. It was eventually called Fort Randall. [2] In October, 1855, Father Trecy paid his first visit to the fort. According to his accounts, he found over 600 Catholics, mostly Irish. They included the commander, General Harney, who had married an Irish Catholic and had been converted to Catholicism. During his stay, Father Trecy heard the confessions of 500 individuals. These Irish-American soldiers and their families should be considered part of the first Irish-American community in the region. The community would remain an important area of Irish settlement until the fort's closing in 1892. The post's Catholics housed various Catholic priests during this period.

In 1855, up the Sioux River from Sioux City in what is present-day Union County, South Dakota, Chris Maloney established a trading post. [3] This post became an important stopping point on the military road from Sioux City to Fort Randall.

During the winter of 1855-56, Bishop Loras sent Father Trecy as his personal envoy to the Irish Emigrant Aid Convention, which began February 12, 1856 in Buffalo, New York. The leading force at the convention was Thomas D'Arcy McGee. McGee was disturbed by what was happening to his fellow Irishmen in the slums of the eastern cities. Like other Irish-American leaders, McGee was upset by the nativistic, Know-Nothing Movement which attempted to harass recent Irish immigrants, and attempted to keep them from securing certain jobs and improved living conditions. At the convention, McGee condemned the selfish activities of Irish-American politicians of the eastern cities.

The people who attended the Irish Emigrant Aid Convention proposed the organization of a joint-stock company that would put up shares to those Irish who were in a position to buy western farm lands jointly and then sell them to prospective settlers. The statement from the convention promised to take the Irish west and give them "the blessing of rural settlement with church and school".

Several members of the American Roman Catholic Church hierarchy, especially Archbishop John Hughes of New York City, considered McGee to be a radical. Trecy, who had played an

Father Jerimiah Trecy directed the establishment of St. John's City in 1856. Courtesy of the Archives of the Archdiocese of Omaha.

influential role in the convention, was publicly attacked by Archbishop Hughes in subsequent speeches and statements to the press. During the following year, 1857, Bishop Loras of Dubuque commissioned Father Trecy to go east for a series of lectures. During one of Trecy's presentations in New York City, Archbishop Hughes, standing up in the crowd, confronted the speaker about his activities to encourage emigration to the West. Archbishop Hughes believed that it was alright for the Irish to go west as individuals. To emigrate to the west in little Catholic groups would make the Irish become as distinct as the Mormons. As a result, they might fall victim to the same kind of harassment suffered by the members of the Mormon religion.[2]

During 1859, St. John City, along with Omaha and Nebraska City, competed for the seat of the Catholic Church's newly-created Vicariate of Nebraska. In the fall of 1860, it was awarded to Omaha. Father Trecy left St. John City after aiding in the successful legal defense of disputed land claims on the settlement. He left to serve as a chaplain during the Civil War. The settlement was later named Jackson, after it moved in 1862 to a more accessible location a few miles to the east. In 1863, several homes and the original church in St. John City were destroyed by a prairie fire. On June 15, 1870, a tornado struck and destroyed the greater share of the remaining buildings.

James McHenry and Michael Ryan from the St. John City settlement would play major roles in the development of various early Irish settlements in Dakota Territory. The Irish contingent at Fort Randall would also make an important contribution.

In 1857, an expedition, which included Irish settlers and was financed by the Western Land Company of Dubuque, laid out a proposed land site near the Falls of the Big Sioux River. [4] Included in the group was Irish-born John McClellan. Dennis Mahoney, at the time the editor of the *Dubuque Herald*, was one of the financial supporters of the expedition.

Various local histories suggest that Mahoney was part of the expedition. In fact, he never visited the site. Mahoney was involved as a representative in the Iowa Legislature and in operating the

Dubuque Herald. He would eventually run for a seat in the U.S. Congress from Iowa.

During the spring of 1859, Michael Ryan (one of the St. John City settlers), William Matthews, and an A. Christi moved into Dakota just north of Chris Maloney's post. [3] George Fiske, Enos Stutsman, and Downer T. Bramble moved to a place along Beaver Creek, six miles north of Yankton. [12] These people were part of the first wave of white settlers allowed into the region after the Yankton Sioux Treaty of 1858 permitted settlement in the region.

While St. John City, which later became Jackson, took root on the south bank of the Missouri, others lined up to take advantage of the opening of the "Yankton Triangle" on the north bank of the Missouri, upstream from Sioux City. Scandinavians from Winona, Minnesota took a Nebraska site as a similar staging area slightly below the mouth of the James River. There they awaited the implementation of the terms of the 1858 Treaty of Washington, by which Yankton Sioux ceded most of present day East River, South Dakota to the United States. Soon after, this land opened for entry.

In 1859, several groups took sites along the Big Sioux River Valley. One such site became the city of Canton. Spearheaded by land speculators Daniel Frost and John B.S. Todd of Sioux City, other groups moved along the lower James River, where Fiske, Stutsman, and Bramble had placed their community at Beaver Creek.

By the middle of 1860, Irish were interspersed among other groups around the perimeter of white settlement on the Yankton Triangle: at St. John's City; at Chris Mahoney's post on the lower Sioux, at the Western Land Company site at the Falls of the Sioux, at the Beaver Creek settlement and with the contingent of American soldiers stationed at Fort Randall.

By 1860, Michael Ryan had established the Twelve Mile House. The village of Jefferson grew up around Ryan's residence. The United States Census of 1860 stated that Margarette Coffee, a widow with three children, had a residence near the Maloney house. Coffee had been born in Ireland. The area was by this time called Big Sioux Point. [5]

By 1860, Mahlon Gore, residing near Deer Point, now the present-day town of Elk Point, attempted a crop of potatoes. His intentions were to supply the soldiers at Fort Randall with an ample supply of the Irish peasants' main staple. His account also recalled a Father Martin preaching a sermon at Michael Ryan's residence.[3]

John Stanage, Irish born and both English and Gaelic speaking, served in the United States Army in California during and after the Mexican-American War. He later was transferred to an army fort along the Missouri River. Stanage mustered out of the U.S. Army at Fort Pierre in 1858. [17] In July of 1859, after serving for a time as a civilian employee at Fort Pierre, Stanage established a trading post along the east bank of the James River, a few miles from the Missouri River. [6] A ferry line crossed the James River just west of Stanage's post. In September, 1860, Henry Bradley settled near John Stanage's residence on the James River. This began further Irish settlement in the area around Stanage's post.

In 1859, James McHenry, also a former St. John's City resident, established a residence at the trading post which had been Fort Vermillion. He established the first store at the post during the winter of 1860-61. [7] McHenry taught the first school in a log cabin called Father Martin's Church. Soon Fort Vermillion was abandoned by all its residents because of physical deterioration and spring time floods along the Missouri Valley. Eventually McHenry located a residence fifteen miles up from the Missouri on the Vermillion River. McHenry's residence would eventually come to be called Bloomingdale. [8]

Eventually, elections were held in 1861 to form the first Dakota Territorial Legislature. James McHenry, John Stanage, Chris Maloney, Michael Ryan, and Enos Stutsman were among the representatives chosen. Bob Karolevitz, in <u>Yankton, A Pioneer Past</u>, describes the humorous antics of this group in the off hours of the legislative session.

In June of 1861, Pat and Mike Curry, Irish born Patrick Brown, and their families, arrived at Elk Point. They established three farms southeast of Elk Point on land around Elk Grove. They were charter members of St. Peter's Catholic Church in Jefferson. Although the

St. Peter's church is usually portrayed as being of French origin, a substantial portion of the congregation, as many thirty five percent in one estimation, were Irish Catholics. The Currys and the Browns participated in the grasshopper treks of the 1870s.

By 1860, Fort Dakota had been established near the falls of the Big Sioux. [9] Residents of the outpost included Margaret Callahan, an Irish born woman; Berne Fowler and his Irish born wife, Marge; and John McClellan. Berne Fowler carried the mail by horseback from Sioux Falls to Yankton. The Dakota Territory census of 1860 stated that McClellan was employed by the Western Land Company and possessed $900 in real estate.[4] His land would eventually play an important role in developing the Irish community of Sioux Falls. In 1861, John McClellan became a member of the Dakota Cavalry stationed at Fort Dakota. John participated in the defense of Fort Dakota when the Minnesota Sioux War of September, 1862 occurred. A Yankton Sioux band led by Smutty Bear attacked John Stanage's post along the James River. Stanage, who had learned to speak Dakota during his years along the river, was instrumental in convincing other Yanktons into not participating in the war.[5]

The Ft. Dakota Military Reserve at the Sioux Falls was the residence of several Irish Americans. Courtesy of the Siouxland Heritage Museums.

Berne and Marge Fowler moved to Yankton during the evacuation of Sioux Falls, and eventually homesteaded north of Yankton.

Irish settlers in Dakota joined local militias formed in response to the Sioux War of 1862. The war created the need for an increased military presence at Fort Randall. Sylvester Delaney served in the militia at Fort Dakota. In 1866, the Delaney family would be one of the four families living in the Sioux River Valley. The last commander of Fort Dakota was John Duffy, who like Delaney, was Irish born. John O'Grady served at Fort Dakota soon after the Sioux War, and in 1868 mustered out of the military at Fort Randall. He traveled to Fort Dakota and homesteaded part of the former military reserve. His homestead was located approximately five miles north of Fort Dakota along the Sioux River.[6]

The Dakota Territory Census of 1860 lists twenty people born in Ireland. Chris Maloney and Margaret Coffee do not appear in any records after the Dakota War of 1862. Maloney may have moved to the area around Fort Randall with other Big Sioux Point people.

The settlement of Irish along the Missouri River in the newly created Dakota Territory coincided with more publicized attempts along the Missouri River in other parts of the American West. James Fisk and Thomas Meagher carried out attempts at Irish settlement in the newly created Montana Territory. The expeditions to Montana crossed Dakota Territory. More importantly, the experiences and reasons for settlement were quite similar to the settlements in Dakota.

Thomas Francis Meagher was a prominent figure in the Young Ireland Movement, which was part of the Irish Uprising of 1848. Like other Young Ireland leaders, Meagher was imprisoned by the British government. He was eventually sent into exile in Australia. While imprisoned in Australia, he escaped and went into permanent exile, taking up residence in the Irish community of New York City in 1852.

Because of his reputation, Meagher became one of the leading spokesmen for the Irish in America. He spoke at many Democratic party functions. In June of 1857, he spoke on "Royalty and

Republicanism", and the life of Daniel O'Connell, in Dubuque, Iowa.[7]

Although he had publicly supported many of the Southern states positions prior to 1861, when the move to secede took place, Meagher chose to support the Republican party's position of preserving the Union. Meagher also believed that Irish Americans could receive training in the war between the states that would be essential in the inevitable war of independence against the British. Meagher was the most prominent Irish American politician to receive a military officer's commission from President Abraham Lincoln at the beginning of the Civil War conflict. Captain Meagher was made commander of the 69th Regiment, New York State Volunteers, an all Irish contingent. The Fighting 69th distinguished themselves in many battles during the war. This performance and the activities of its commander made Thomas Meagher one of the most prominent Irishmen in America.[8]

James Fisk, a wealthy Irish American, was involved in the promotion of expeditions to the gold fields of the Yellowstone country of Montana. "Minnesota to Montana" and "Ho For the Gold Fields" were two slogans of Fisk's campaign. Working out of St. Paul, Fisk led several attempts at reaching the Montana gold fields. In 1864, twelve people from one of Fisk's expeditions were killed near present-day Bowman County, North Dakota by Lakota people under the leadership of Sitting Bull. The expedition was driven to and laid siege upon at Fort Dilts, Dakota Territory.

During the summer of 1865, James Fisk had returned to St. Paul and was carrying out further promotional activities. On July 23, 1865, Thomas Meagher, captain of the recently retired Irish Brigade, arrived in St. Paul in response to a special invitation by James Fisk. Soon after his arrival in St. Paul, Meagher was asked to speak at a gathering in his honor. In his speech, Meagher stated that he had come "West" to improve his condition in life.

He stated that it had been painful for himself to see his fellow Irishmen living in the "squalor of larger cities when they might come to such new fields of opportunity as the West could furnish." He also hoped to set an example to other former Irish American soldiers by giving up the life of a soldier for the quiet life of a family man.

Soon after his initial speech in St. Paul, Meagher was invited by Father John Ireland, a resident pastor in St. Paul and president of the Minnesota Irish Emmigration Society, to speak at a fundraising gathering. In his speech for the Emmigration Society, Meagher once again expressed pity for the plight of the Irish in the slums of the eastern cities. Meagher stated that he hoped to colonize Montana with Irish Catholics. He promised to make every effort to get more priests for Montana territory, and would make every effort to get a bishop appointed for Montana. Within the jurisdictional structure of the Catholic Church, all of the land west of the Missouri River was part of the Vicariate of Nebraska under the supervision of Bishop James O'Connor of Omaha. Word of these statements did not sit well with Bishop O'Connor. The Vicariate of Nebraska eventually did provide missionaries to Montana.[9]

On the evening of the speech before the Immigration Society, Meagher received word that he had been appointed Secretary of Montana by President Andrew Johnson. The contents of Meagher's speech were relayed to the various Irish American newspapers in the East. The newspapers condemned Meagher's "new political creed". They were especially upset with his views that the recently freed Negroes had a right to full citizenship.

Meagher journeyed to Montana Territory by traveling down the Mississippi River and back up the Missouri River. At Atkinson, Kansas he declined an invitation by the local Fenian organization to speak at a gathering. He traveled by stage from Kansas through Denver to Salt Lake City. From Salt Lake City, he rode by stage to Virginia City, Montana. Because of the absence of Montana's governor, Sidney Edgerton, Meagher became the acting governor of Montana Territory.

This account will not detail all of Meagher's activities in Montana. Several events in Meagher's experience related to the activities of Irish people in Dakota.

A majority of the residents of Montana were from the southern states and their political affiliation was Democrat. Meagher's

Republican and Civil War hero background did not sit well with his constituents. His plans to create Irish colonies were not well received.

Because of Meagher's previous statements about Irish Americans learning the ways of war in order to prepare for an armed revolt against England, Meagher was mentioned at various times as being involved in the Fenian attacks on Canada in 1866. He publicly denied any involvement with O'Neill's excursions into Canada. The author has not encountered any mention of his involvement.

The one incident that symbolized the conflict between the acting governor of Montana and its citizens was the Daniels affair. James Daniels, an Irish American, was involved in a shooting spree following a card game dispute. After his conviction, he had been sentenced to three years in jail by the Vigilance Committee of Helena. After three weeks of incarceration, Daniels was pardoned by fellow countryman and acting governor, Thomas Meagher. Meagher was accused of granting the pardon while "under the influence of an unfortunate habit". Federal Judge Lyman Munson attempted to get the pardon rescinded. Meagher refused. To make things worse, Daniels returned to Helena and threatened the people who had testified against him. Soon after, Daniels was strung up to a nearby tree by the vigilantes of Helena. Pinned to his coat was the message, "If our acting governor does this again, we will hang him too."[10] This incident probably influenced the attitude of the federal government officials toward cases such as those of William Barry and Jack McCall that later occurred in Dakota.

In July of 1866, Green Clay Smith was appointed to succeed Edgerton as governor of Montana Territory. Meagher returned to his post as secretary. In the fall of 1866, Meagher failed in his attempt at receiving federal money to raise an army to fight the northern plains Indians.

In the spring of 1867, Meagher traveled by river boat from Virginia City to Fort Benton. Meagher became severely ill, perhaps because of the severe heat on the journey. Recalling that he had been threatened by the residents of Fort Benton previously, Meagher accepted lodging on the boat, *G.A. Thompson,* captained by an old acquaintance, Johnny Doran, rather than in a hotel near Fort Benton. That evening a sentry on board Doran's vessel saw a white figure and then heard a loud splash. The person disappeared into the Missouri River. Thomas Meagher's body was never recovered. It was suggested by some that he was drunk at the time of his drowning. Thomas Meagher never succeeded in establishing an organized colonial scheme in Montana Territory. Meagher, the most recognized Irish politician of the time, would suffer a tragic death during his attempt at creating settlements in the West.

Successful settlements, in contrast, continued to be established in Dakota Territory. During 1868, Dennis Carroll, Patrick Jennings and wife; and John and Brigit Maher settled in Union County, Dakota. The community they formed was called Emmet in honor of the Irish patriot, Robert Emmet. [10] By 1871, there were at least twenty-one families attending the local Catholic services. In 1873, the first Catholic church, St. Joseph, was built on land donated by Patrick Reedy. By this time the settlers at Emmet numbered twenty-seven families with each family averaging ten children.[11]

The first church from this area to appear in the Catholic directory was St. Columban of Brule Creek. This church would become St.

The first church and residence at the Emmet settlement was built in 1873. Courtesy of the Archives of the Diocese of Sioux Falls.

Mary and the community called Garryowen. [11] Vicariate of Nebraska priests, including Fathers James Ryan, Felix McLaughlin, E.P. Walters, and Edward Dillon, ministered to the Catholics at Fort Randall, Vermillion, the French Settlement and along the James River. Emmet was considered the northernmost parish of the Omaha Diocese. To the south of Emmet, in 1869, Irish born John Walsh established a homestead five miles east of Elk Point in Union County. "Honest John" was eventually elected to the Dakota Territorial Legislature.

In 1868, William, James and Edward Dwyer homesteaded to the north and west of Emmet. This community became Lodi. The first church at Lodi was called St. Patrick's. Another Dwyer brother, Thomas, spent time in the community before moving to California. It has been suggested that the name for the town of Lodi, California came from Thomas Dwyer.

Events during the years 1868 through 1872 were conducive to increased immigration. Over the previous decade, the Yankton Triangle had been plagued by the Minnesota Sioux War, occasional

The Bloomingdale Mill, built by James McHenry, was located approximately 19 miles from the mouth of the Vermillion River, on the road east from the Missouri River forts. Courtesy of the South Dakota Historical Society.

floods, and a major drought with accompanying grasshopper plagues. The Sioux refrained from an armed reaction to increase settlement during this period. Moisture returned to the Great Plains with no floods occurring.

By 1868, James McHenry had carried out the construction of a dam on the Vermillion River at Bloomingdale. Soon after, a flour mill was constructed. [8] The road from the Missouri forts to the east ran through Bloomingdale. Father R. Boucher visited the settlement in August, 1869. He counted seventeen Catholic farmers, only two of which had families. Boucher's account noted that a Mrs. Jones, the mother-in-law of James McHenry, had pledged land and money to build a church if Boucher, or another missionary priest, would establish a mission church in the Bloomingdale settlement.[12]

The House of the Dakota Territory Legislature of 1867-68 included Mike Ryan from Union County, William Brady, Caleb Cummings, and James Keegan. Also in the Legislature was Enos Stutsman. Stutsman was of old American stock and not Irish. However, he would play an important role among the Irish Americans in the next years.

In 1869, Father Pierre DeSmet wrote fellow missionary Asa Curtis in Omaha. DeSmet stated, "We may then determine the possibility of visiting the French Settlement between Sioux City and Yankton. They inhabit a rich and beautiful country. No valley along the Missouri exceeds its richness in soil."[13] In 1869, Father Ferdinand Lechleitner served the Catholics living on the Dakota side of the Missouri. Only a few Catholics lived in Yankton. The greatest concentration was ten miles from St. Helena, Nebraska, at the mouth of the James River. This was the location of John Stanage's settlement. Father Lechleitner's main responsibility was to serve the forts along the Missouri and care for the Catholic Native Americans. The largest number of Catholics in Dakota Territory at the time were among the Native Americans, French people to the north around Ft. Pembina, and the Irish Americans stationed at the Missouri River forts. In correspondence to his superior, Omaha Bishop James O'Connor, Father Lechleitner expressed his disappointment in not securing money to establish a mission dwelling in Yankton.[14] [12]

Downer T. Bramble's residence was used as the location for an occasional mass. Lechleitner took up temporary residence in a hotel. He was quite upset about the drunkenness of the hotel proprietor, Bradley, an Irish American, and his fellow tenants. Lechleitner made note of the fact that his potential support for construction of a mission church was greatest among General Stanley and the various Irish Catholic officers of the Missouri River forts. Lechleitner's successor in Yankton, Valentine Sommeriesen, left Yankton to provide to the needs of General George Custer's troops in October of 1873. He later joined the Yellowstone Expedition after traveling alone by horse and buggy through Indian territory.

The year 1869 saw the establishment of an Irish American newspaper in Sioux City called the *Evening Times*. Owners of the paper were Charles Collins and E.W. Caldwell. [13] The main reporter for the *Times* was John Brennan. The popularity of attempting to create a successful Irish American newspaper in the 1860s was widespread. Irish Americans viewed the reading and publishing of newspapers as a means for expressing their sense of nationalism in their new homeland.

John Brennan had emigrated from Ireland in 1865 and had spent his first four years in America working as a laborer. He had been in Omaha prior to his arrival in Sioux City in 1869. Nothing is known about Collins prior to his arrival in Sioux City in 1869. Both Brennan and Collins would play a major role in the Irish communities of the region. [15]

Collins' account of his activities during this time mentioned an important trip to St. Louis during the fall of 1869, to the National Convention of the Fenian Brotherhood. [16] This was most likely the National Colonization Convention which met in October, 1869 in St. Louis. Meeting organizers were Dillon O'Brien of St. Paul and William Onahan of Chicago. Mayor Edward O'Neill of Milwaukee presided during the meeting. Several committees were appointed from among the distinguished Irish Americans at the meeting. According to William Onahan, nothing came of the meeting. The idea of an organized colonization operation would be addressed within the decade by Onahan, Dillon O'Brien, and Bishops John

Ireland, James O'Connor, and John Spalding. According to Collins, he and John Pope Hodnett developed a scheme to create an Irish American colony in Dakota Territory. Allegedly, a committee including P.W. Dunne, John Scanlan and other convention members was formed to visit Dakota during the next year to find a suitable location.

According to Collins, national household names such as A.T. Stewart, Jim Fiske Jr., Colonel W. R. Roberts, P.W. Dunne, Ben Butler and Wendell Phillips were backers of the project. A.T. Stewart, a New York department store owner, had an income in 1864 of five million dollars. In Collins' Black Hills Directory and Directory for 1878-79 he states that a bill "authorizing the establishment of a National Colony Bank and colony corporation" was passed by Congress. The records of the second session of the 41st Congress revealed a different set of events. H.R. 1663 was introduced by Senator Logan to incorporate the Irish Colonization Association on March 31, 1870. It was referred to the committee on Public Lands. The bill died in committee. The bill did not propose the creation of a colony and colony bank. Also, none of the household names Collins mentioned appear among the incorporators other than P.W. Dunne of Peoria, Illinois. Charles Collins of Sioux City and John Pope Hodnett, William M. Hodnett, Daniel O'Farrell, and William Bodkin of Yankton, Dakota Territory were among the associates.

The most noteworthy person listed as both an associate and member of the board was New York newspaper publisher, Horace Greeley. Greeley was involved in another colonization scheme during this time with Nathan Meeker, the education editor of Greeley's New York Tribune. This effort produced the "Union Colony" in Colorado. In 1870, Meeker would rename the colony Greeley.[17] Greeley was quite elderly and in poor health in 1870. He had been the personal target of many Irish rioters during the anti-draft riots of 1863 in New York City. Perhaps after the horrible experience of the 1863 riots, Greeley developed the belief, like many others of this time, that the plight of the inner-city, slum Irish could be improved by movement to the West.

John Pope Hodnett of Chicago was appointed Assessor of Internal Revenue for the District of Dakota Territory in April of 1869. Hodnett was only around thirty years of age at the time of his appointment by Republican President Grant. The Civil War led some Irish Americans to abandon the traditional Democratic Party and become "Irish Republicans". Hodnett appears to have been the darling of this group. He was identified as a member of the "O'Neill" faction of the Fenians. He was evidently an excellent public speaker and somewhat well known nationally prior to his appointment. Charles Collins claimed that he had met Hodnett at the Fenian Convention in St. Louis in 1869. For certain, Hodnett did travel to Dakota and established a homestead claim seven miles north of Yankton. [12] According to Kingsbury's History of South Dakota, he planted orchards, grain fields and "brilliant gardens". He called his place, Lake Lalla Rookh. Apparently Hodnett dammed a stream on his homestead.[18]

According to Collins they traveled the summer of 1869 up the Missouri River to the mouth of the White River as members of the Irish Colonization Association. In the August 16, 1907 issue of the *Sioux Falls Daily Press*, Dan Scott, in response to an editorial entitled "Fragments of History", stated that Charley Collins, John Brennan, Tom Hodnett, Dan Hodnett, and John Pope Hodnett traveled to the Brule City location in order to secure the area for the Irish settlement. According to Scott, Collins had collected a large amount of cash to secure the location from its resident, Jim Somers. Dan Hodnett, a "successful sporting man in those days", challenged Somers to gamble for the control of the site. Hodnett succeeded in winning the card game. But according to Scott, Somers proceeded to hold a "brace of guns" on Tom Hodnett, forcing him to throw up his "hand" and head quickly down the river bottom. Somers retained control of the site. In August, 1870, Hodnett met with Omaha's Catholic Bishop James O'Gorman in Yankton. Reports stated that they discussed the possibilities of Irish settlement in Southeastern Dakota.[19]

According to Collins, a committee from the 1869 Fenian Convention rendezvoused in Sioux City during the summer of 1870.

They took a boat from Sioux City to Yankton. From Yankton to the mouth of the White River, the committee traveled by wagons. The Great Plains were suffering through a drought that summer. One can imagine the committee arriving at the proposed site in the heat of midsummer. According to Charles Collins, the committee submitted a majority report against this colonization effort. The minority report was in favor of establishing a colony to be named Limerick. This site would become Charles Collins's boom town of Brule City. [19]

According to the *Sioux City Journal* of October 26, 1870, John Hodnett departed Dakota after being "assailed". Hodnett had been a partner with Dennis Mahoney of the Western Land Company in the Dubuque, Iowa *Herald* beginning in 1860. In 1870, Dennis Mahoney, Stilson Hutchins, and John Hodnett established the *St. Louis Daily Times*. Mahoney served as editor and proprietor for about fifteen months. Mahoney sold out his partnership and returned to Dubuque in 1871.

The November 17, 1870 *Journal* noted that Episcopal lobbyist, William Welch had gone to Washington D.C. Welch convinced President Grant to annul a declaration opening the lands north of the Military Reserve at Fort Randall and the Yankton Reservation to settlement. This was done at the insistence of Brule Lakota leader Spotted Tail, whose people were at the Whetstone Agency north of Fort Randall. The purpose was to prevent the further sale of liquor to the Indians. President Grant responded by establishing a "presidential addition". The land was placed under military control and settlement was prohibited. By doing so, the Brule City settlement was curtailed.

The idea of creating Irish colonies in the West was discussed among the Irish Americans in the 1860s. Irish colonization into Dakota would intensify in the 1870s. The activities of Irish Nationalists, as part of the Fenian movement, would take place within the region.

1   Henry Casper, S. J., History of the Catholic Church in Nebraska (Bruce Press, Milwaukee, 1960), Pages 3-22.

2   Ironically, a group of Mormons, led by James Emmett, spent parts of 1845-46 near the mouth of the Vermillion River, in the vicinity of Fort Vermillion which was at that time on the property of the Yankton Sioux band chief Mad Bull. It later became part of Dakota Territory. It is quite unlikely that Bishop Loras was aware of this situation, however. Richard Bennett, "Mormon Renegade: James Emmett at the Vermillion, 1846", South Dakota State Historical Society Quarterly (Volume 15, No.3, Fall, 1985, Pierre, South Dakota), Pages 217 -233.

3   E. Frank Peterson, Peterson's Illustrated Atlas of South Dakota, Vermillion, 1904.

4   "Dakota Census of 1860", South Dakota Historical Collections (1925, Pierre, South Dakota), Pages 396-439

5   John Stanage Family History Notes.

6   Notes on Fort Dakota, David Rambow Collection, Pipestone, Minnesota.

7   Robert G. Athearn, Thomas Francis Meagher: An Irish Revolutionary in America (U. of Colorado Press, Boulder, 1949), Pages 89-109, 142-171.

8   Robert G. Athearn, Thomas Francis Meagher: An Irish Revolutionary in America (U. of Colorado Press, Boulder, 1949), Pages 89 -109, 142-171.

9   Henry Casper, S.J., History of the Catholic Church in Nebraska (Bruce Press, Milwaukee, 1960), Page 221.

10   Robert G. Athearn, Thomas Francis Meagher: An Irish Revolutionary in America (U. of Colorado Press, Boulder, 1949), Page 151.

11   Father J.P. Leen, History of St. Joseph's Church, Emmet, (1946).

12   Archives of the Archdiocese of Omaha, Letter from Father R. Boucher to Bishop James O'Gorman, August, 1869.

13   Henry Casper, S.J., History of the Catholic Church in Nebraska (Bruce Press, Milwaukee, 1960), Pages 237-238.

14   Archives of the Archdiocese of Omaha, Letter from Ferdinand

Lechlietner to Bishop James O'Gorman, October, 1869.

15   Charles Collins is often portrayed as the only Irishman in the region attempting to organize Irish settlements. This was not the case. Among several South Dakota historians, the idea of an Irish settlement in the territory is considered a wild hair, "preposterous as it seems". There were, in fact, several, successful Irish settlements in the Territory. The question must be asked why Irish settlement in Minnesota, Iowa, Nebraska, and Montana is accepted as part of the common pattern of American settlement in the region, while in South Dakota it is portrayed as a foolish endeavor. It is true that Charles Collins carried out various activities in Dakota. However, if one were to weigh the importance of one's contribution on the the amount of mention one receives, people such as the John Brennans', John Stanage, and James McHenry would receive much more historical mention than Charles Collins.

16   Charles Collins, Collins' History and Directory of the Black Hills, 1878-79 (Sioux City, 1879).

17   William Harlan Hale, Horace Greeley, Voice of the People (New York, 1947), Pages 309-310.

18   George Kingsbury, Kingsbury's History of South Dakota (Pierre, South Dakota, 1915), S.J. Clarke Co. Chicago, Pages 526-527.

19   Robert Karolevitz, Pioneer Church in Pioneer City (North Plains Press, Aberdeen, South Dakota, 1972), Page 13.

CHAPTER 2

FENIAN ACTIVITY IN
DAKOTA TERRITORY

Three important historical events in the 1860's would greatly influence Irish settlement in Dakota. The events began with the organization of the Fenian Brotherhood and the group's activities following the Civil War. In Dakota Territory the seizure of Fort Pembina and the murder trial of William Barry brought attention to Irish activities in the region. Nearly a million Irish had emigrated to America during and after the Great Famine.

These emigrants continued to believe in the cause of Irish Nationalism. Among the Irish were formed organizations dedicated to bringing about an armed revolt against the British control of Ireland. The Fenian Brotherhood was organized in the years preceding the Civil War. Two of the major organizers were James Stephens and John O'Mahony. Stephens was considered the political organizer. O'Mahony, a scholar of Celtic history, was considered the political theorist. O'Mahony believed that the horrible situation that the Irish people found themselves in was the result of a sentimental clinging to past glory. Allegiance to the tribal, clan, political system had led to Ireland's failure to successfully resist the conquest by England.

He proposed the creation of a new, nationalist organization to carry out an organized, rebellion against English rule. O'Mahony, being the Gaelic scholar, suggested that the movement be named for the mythical, Gaelic warriors, Fianna. Another of the beliefs held by Irish Nationalists was that the true possessors of the land of Ireland were the Irish peasants. The system of landholdings imposed by the British were to be rejected. Ireland's land was to be returned to the peasant's possession, held in common trust, in a common spirit of national identity.[1]

By 1862 Fenian organizations flourished among Irish American soldiers of the Union Army. The Irish immigrants were receiving excellent training in the Civil War. Experience that could be quite helpful in a revolution in Ireland.

By 1865, James Stephens, operating underground in Ireland, claimed that nearly 85,000 men were organized in Ireland in preparation for an uprising. The leadership of the Fenian Brotherhood was unable to decide whether to carry out military actions against the English in Ireland or against British forces in Canada. Members of the Fenian Central Council included Henry C. McCarthy and Michael Scanlan of Chicago, Peter Dunne of Peoria, Illinois, James Gibbon of Philadelphia, William Sullivan of Tiffin, Ohio, Brigadier General Smyth of the Army of the Cumberland, Patrick Bannon of Louisville, James Meehan and William Roberts of New York, and William Griffin of Madison, Indiana. Michael Scanlan and William F. Roberts were eventually selected to the Fenian Senate. John Pope Hodnett was nominated but not chosen for one of the cabinet positions in the Fenian provisional government.

Several instances of small, armed resistance against the British occurred in Ireland in the first months of 1867. Several soldiers were imprisoned in Ireland as a result of these incidents. Three Fenians were executed for their involvement. They were William Allen, Michael Larkin, and Michael O'Brien, later called the "Manchester Martyrs". One of the priests who gave these three Irish Catholics their last rites was Father Thomas Quick. Father Quick would later serve as a priest of the Catholic diocese of Sioux Falls. He is buried in Flandreau, South Dakota.[2] [64]

Also imprisoned after the Fenian incidents of 1867 were Jerimiah O'Donavan Rossa, John Martin, James Stevens, Edward Duffy, and Edward's brother, John T. Duffy. John T. Duffy and Rossa were imprisoned for one and a half years. Edward Duffy died in prison. John T. Duffy emigrated to Dakota Territory in the 1880's and died April 30,1914, in North Dakota.[3]

The events of 1867 were Fenian responses to activities in America during the previous year. By the spring of 1866 troops pledged to the Fenian cause were organized at various points near the Canadian and American border. It is estimated that approximately thirty five thousand men under General T.W.

The experiences and subsequent executions of the "Manchester Martyrs" inspired the composition, <u>God Save Ireland</u>. Reprinted by permission of Little, Brown & Co., and the Library of Congress.

Sweeney were prepared for an invasion of Canada. Included in this group were forces under John O'Neill located near Buffalo, New York. Sweeney had served as a major and later as a brevet general in the Union army. He served as the secretary of war of the Irish Republic. Sweeney had suggested that General Philip Sheridan be offered command of the Fenian forces. Apparently Sheridan did not receive an offer or declined the offer that he had been tendered. The American Fenian Brotherhood was split over the issue of invading Canada. William W. Roberts and members of the Fenian Senate favored an invasion. Supporters of O'Mahony believed that armed resistance should take place only in Ireland.

On St. Patrick's Day, March 17, 1866, Governor Marshall of Minnesota and Bishop Grace of St. Paul gave speeches condemning Fenian activities during a celebration in St. Paul.

On May 30, 1866, detachments of "Fenian" soldiers, dressed in newly designed, green Fenian uniforms and flying the Fenian Brotherhood flag, crossed over from Buffalo and landed in British territory. The Fenian soldiers seized property near Fort Erie, Ontario. A division of four hundred men under John O'Neill's command met a British force at Ridgeway, Canada. The ensuing battle resulted in a victory by O'Neill's Fenian troops. A second battle at nearby Limestone Ridge resulted in a second victory by O'Neill's men. Fenian reinforcements were located across Lake Erie, outside of Buffalo, New York. O'Neill moved to Fort Erie and secured positions to await further reinforcements. By this time messages of the successful victories by the Fenian troops had reached members of Andrew Johnson's administration in Washington, D.C. Fenian leaders believed that once presented with such a situation President Johnson would turn his head away and let the Fenian soldiers carry out their plans. This did not, however, occur. President Johnson issued a proclamation calling for the Fenian soldiers as American citizens to disperse and return home. He also ordered General George Meade, military commander of U.S. forces in the Buffalo area to prevent further reinforcements to cross over into Canada. Realizing the situation, John O'Neill and his troops surrendered to the American army at Fort Niagara. None of the Fenian soldiers were arrested. General Meade recommended that the American government pay for train transportation for the Fenians away from Buffalo. The Fenian army dispersed without incident.[4] Michael Scanlan was among the Fenian leaders arrested by the American government after the invasion. He was released before receiving formal charges.

A few months after the incursion into Canada, John O'Neill was appointed inspector general of the Irish Republican Army. By 1867, O'Neill had succeeded William W. Roberts as president of the Fenian Brotherhood. The Fenian leadership believed that actions in America would in some manner affect British economic activities. More specifically, they believed that if a large number of British armies were forced to become involved in an armed conflict in the central part of America, they could not respond sufficiently to an armed revolt in Ireland. They believed that "England's difficulty is Ireland's opportunity". John O'Neill continued to address crowds

John O'Neill, Civil War officer, Fenian and colonization leader. Courtesy of the Archives of the Archdiocese of Omaha.

urging them to support the invasion of Canada by the Fenian forces. The arms purchased for the 1866 invasion, and later seized by the American government, were returned to the Fenian officials after the election of 1866.

In an address on December 8, 1876, nine years after the first Fenian attack into Canada, a speech delivered several times across the United States, John O'Neill explained the rationale for these military actions.[5]

"I have always believed in striking at England wherever we could reach her and wherever the English flag floats and the English government is recognized and there are English soldiers in arms to defend the flag and maintain the government. I hold that the Irish people, particularly the Irish exiles who her oppressive laws have driven from their native land have a right to go there and make war on England. No doubt she would much prefer having them make war nearer home where she could much more readily concentrate her forces and crush them out, but it is high time that Irish patriots who claim to be revolutionaries should learn to act not as England desires but in the way best calculated to serve their own purpose. If we could meet England at a disadvantage at the North Pole that in my judgment would be the best place to strike her. There is no spot on earth I would rather fight England than on Irish soil, but if it is not practicable to fight there then I am in favor of fighting her wherever we can reach her. There is a long line of British frontier between Nova Scotia and VanCouver's Island with the Atlantic and Pacific Oceans as an outlet and there are millions of the Irish race in the United States from whom to recruit an army and man privateers to pray on the British commerce and I imagine if Hugh O'Neill or Owen Roe, Patrick Sarsfield, Wolf Tone, Lord

Edward Fitzgerald, or Robert Emmett were living in America today it would not be long before an Irish army would be encamped on British soil with the green flag floating over it. Fellow countrymen there is not one of you I know who does not feel pride in the achievements of these heroes of the past but are you on who devolves the responsibility of defending the cause for which these patriots fought and bled and died ready to perform your duty to Mother Ireland as they performed theirs? If so England can soon be made to tremble for North American possessions and her commerce on the high seas."

This address was made during the time that John O'Neill had established residence in the O'Neill Colony in northcentral Nebraska. O'Neill would lead a third attack of Canada from Dakota Territory. This would be one of many related events in the next decade to occur in Dakota.

The Fenian movement was well organized among the Irish settlers of Iowa. Following the Civil War, Fenian circles were formed through the region. In April, 1866, a Fenian meeting was held in Des Moines. The Iowa State Register was considered pro-Irish and anti-British. The Fenian attacks on Canada were supported by many of the Iowa publications. Large Fenian demonstrations were held in Dubuque as part of the July 4, 1866 celebration. Fenian supporters from Iowa, Wisconsin, and Minnesota held a convention in Dubuque, from July 2 to July 4, 1867. The Fenian Brotherhood met in Dubuque again in 1868. Speakers were Professor Brophy of Washington, D.C., and General John O'Neill, by that time President of the Fenian Brotherhood. The *Chicago Irish Republic*, edited by Michael Scanlan, and a major mouthpiece for the Fenian movement, had 5,000 subscribers in Iowa in 1868. W.S. Burke of the *Council Bluffs Nonpariel* was sent to report on the Fenian invasions first hand.[6]

Henry O'Connor became Attorney General of Iowa in 1867. He was considered a major spokesman for the Fenians in the region.

The National Irish Republican Convention was held in Chicago on July 5, 1869. O'Connor was chosen a member of the National Executive Committee. He was defeated by Michael Scanlan, of Chicago, for the chairmanship by two votes.

Pro-Fenian sentiment most likely prevailed among the Irish American soldiers stationed at the military posts along the Missouri River. By 1867, Fenian circles with names such as the Emeralds, Shamrocks, and the Phoenix were organized in Omaha. Each had a military branch. Recruiting of members was quite successful. The *Sioux City Daily Times* during the last days of December, 1869 detailed the establishment of the Wolfe Tone Circle of the Fenian Brotherhood. The Circle consisted of twenty five members and quickly established a hall and martial band. Bishop James O'Gorman of Omaha, was aware of the organizations, considered to be secret societies, but did not officially condemn the involvement of Irish Catholics in the organizations.[7]

The murder case of William Barry would bring to initial public attention the presence of Fenian sentiment in the region. On the night of June 7-8, 1867, a British military officer, Wilfred Speer, was murdered on the Missouri River steamboat, *Texas*, on the river below Fort Buford. Although the soldiers on the boat were not on full military status to guard the vessel, there was a sentry on duty. His name was William Barry, an acknowledged member of the Fenian Brotherhood. Barry was immediately detained by his commanding officer, P.W. Horrigan. However, his superiors soon released Barry. The authorities decided that the killing took place while in the line of duty.

A few months later, after complaints from British government authorities and the publishing of a twelve page pamphlet on the case in England, Barry was arrested and taken to Yankton for trial. Requests from the British government for information on the case to United States Secretary of State William Seward, and later Hamilton Fish, kept attention focused on the case. Barry was again released due to a lack of available material witnesses. Joseph LaBarge, the pilot of the *Texas*, had disappeared. After continual complaints from the British government, Barry was arrested another time in Montana in July, 1869. He was taken to the Dakota territorial capital in Yankton for trial once again.

The case against William Barry was finally brought to a jury at Vermillion in November, 1870. [7] Officer Horrigan was not available as a witness. After five days of testimony, the case went to the jury on the evening of November 11, 1870.[8] After being out about one half hour, the jury brought in a verdict of not guilty. The *Sioux City Times'* account stated that after the verdict was announced, the "enthusiasm was great, and the prisoner, counsel, and many spectators were affected to tears. The prisoner was discharged, and before he could get out of the courtroom was seized by his friends who were nearly wild in their enthusiastic congratulations." The *Times* reporter, perhaps John Brennan or Charley Collins, believed this the "greatest trial Dakota ever knew".

Defense attorney, Bartlett Tripp, told the Yankton Press later that Horrigan had brought a mistress along for the journey up the Missouri. Apparently Speer had struck a friendship that Horrigan did not appreciate. Tripp believed that Horrigan had ordered William Barry, the sentry on duty, to shoot anyone who came on deck of the *Texas* after a certain time in the evening. Horrigan knew full well that Speer would be prowling around the deck in the dark. Speer was shot by Barry as a result of the orders of his commanding officer, Horrigan.

William B. O'Donoghue's involvement in the the Metis Rebellion in Rupert's Land on the northern border of Dakota Territory would bring further Fenian activity to the region. Born in County Sligo, Ireland in 1843 William B. O'Donaghue was one of the nearly one million Irishmen to immigrate to America after the Great Famine of 1845-49. Arriving in New York as a young man, O'Donoghue became active in the Fenian movement. After high school he went to Winnipeg, in what was then called Rupert's Land, to attend St. Boniface College. He hoped to become a teacher and study for the priesthood. In 1868 O'Donoghue came in contact with Louis Riel, leader of the half breed or Metis Rebellion.[9]

In 1848, Father George Belcourt, a Roman Catholic priest, had been driven out of the Selkirk settlement of the Hudson's Bay

Company. Father Belcourt had sided with the Metis in a dispute over the right of free trade. He established the settlement of Metis and Chippewa at a post south of the international border, in American territory. After a flood in 1851, Belcourt and Norman Kittson, the local fur trader choose a site thirty miles west of the original site. The new settlement, on Pembina Mountain, was called St. Joseph. [18] It is the site of present-day Walhalla, North Dakota. The settlement included a chapel, school, and a convent of the Sisters of the Propagation of the Faith, a religious community made up of Metis women. It was the brain child of George Belcourt.[10]

Pembina and St. Joseph were considered important American outposts by those American expansionists interested in the possible annexation of Rupert's Land. Prior to Minnesota statehood in 1858, the region was part of Minnesota Territory. All goods shipped out of the region had to travel the water route to St. Paul and the Mississippi River. By 1866, American politicians, such as James W. Taylor, were proposing the construction of a railroad from St. Paul to the Pembina and Winnipeg area. Such a move they believed would win the local population over to the idea of being taken over by the American government.

The Metis were French speaking people of French and Indian ancestry. They were for all extensive purposes independent and self-governing. They were Roman Catholics. Their lifestyle included leaving their homes on the Red River of the North each summer and going out on Buffalo hunts. By 1869, the Metis were hoping to form their own independent government free from control by the British. They were apprehensive of the "anti-papist" attitudes among the English speaking Canadians. More importantly, the Metis were concerned about the preservation of their land rights in any organized Canadian Federation. At this time the Canadian provinces were attempting to form a union of the various territories. It was Louis Riel and his followers' goal to resist any attempts at uniting Rupert's Land, then a colony under the control of the Hudson's Bay Company, with any other of the provinces. During 1869, jurisdiction of the British colony of Rupert's Land, lying directly north of Dakota Territory, was transferred from the Hudson's Bay Company to the newly formed Canadian government. William McDougall was appointed to be the governor of the territory, which would be administered from the government offices in Ottawa.

In response to these actions the Metis under Riel's leadership, formed the National Committee of the Metis of the Red River. William O'Donoghue left his seminary studies to become the treasurer and second in command of Riel's provisional government.

Advising the newly formed Committee at their strategy sessions were Americans, Enos Stutsman and Oscar Malmros. Stutsman, at this time was the chairman of the Dakota Territory Legislature. The Legislature met every other year. As a result, Stutsman was able to maintain property in Yankton and at the same time accept a political appointment to serve as a special revenue agent at Pembina, Dakota Territory. Oscar Malmros served as the United States consul in Winnipeg. The consulate was established in 1867 by a bill introduced by Minnesota United States Senator, Alexander Ramsey. Ramsey was a friend of Malmros and, like Oscar, an ardent expansionist.

Officials of the National Committee of the Metis of the Red River; Louis Riel is seated in the center of the front row. W. B. O'Donoghue is seated to his left. Fellow Fenian, Red O'Lone is seated on the floor to Riel's right. Courtesy of the Provincial Archives of Manitoba.

According to the 1860 census, Pembina had the largest population of any community in Dakota Territory. The community was quite colorful, with its assortment of fur trading post characters. Pembina, as previously noted, was located on the border between the British possession of Rupert's Land and the United States. Stutsman was assigned to try to stop the smuggling of goods into the United States.[11]

On October 11, 1869, a group of Metis led by Louis Riel ordered a Canadian government survey team to leave land owned by the Metis. They claimed that the land belonged to the Metis people. At the same time, William McDougall was traveling up the Red River through Dakota Territory to begin his job as Governor of Rupert's Land. The National Committee quickly organized on a formal basis. A barricade was placed on the border and McDougall was ordered not to enter the Metis land. Enos Stutsman became involved in the attempt to keep McDougall out of his post. Eventually, Louis Riel and the Metis National Committee seized the Hudson's Bay Post at Fort Garry. A provisional government was announced. The provisional government did not receive the support of the English speaking people of Rupert's Land. During the final session of the convention to form the full provisional government, Enos Stutsman proposed that the Metis consider the possibility of their lands being annexed by the United States. A person who expressed support for this idea was, at the time, second in command of Riel's provisional government. He was the Fenian leader, W.B. O'Donaghue. One account states that O'Donaghue shared power with Riel. He made certain that the flag of the provisional government included an Irish shamrock.

William McDougall attempted various means in order to establish control of Rupert's Land. This included appeals to the English speaking population and the recruitment of Native American people to aid in his efforts. Enos Stutsman used these recruitment efforts to create fears of impending attacks by the Native Americans of the region. It is suggested that this was done as possible justification for eventual seizure of the region by United States military forces in order to prevent Indian attacks.

Louis Riel was visited by various emissaries from the Canadian government and by individual residents with connections with the Canadian government. Riel received a Christmas visit from Dr. Charles Tupper and an early January visit from Hudson's Bay official, Donald Smith. Tupper is considered one of the "Fathers of Confederation", and later served as the Canadian prime minister. Smith came as a special, secret representative of the Canadian government. Their visits, along with efforts by Winnipeg resident, Joseph Lemay, apparently convinced Riel not to become involved with the Fenian efforts and the American annexation plans of Stutsman and Malmros. Lemay encouraged Riel to consider British Crown Colony status for Rupert's Land outside the Canadian Confederation. This was the position of many French Canadian Catholic Church clergy. Riel saw this as a means for uniting both the French and English people of the region. Riel continued to involve W.B. O'Donaghue, Red O'Lone, a saloon owner and Fenian supporter, and Stutsman in his negotiating activities. Perhaps Riel viewed the Fenian support and annexation option as means of last resort. Through the efforts of Lemay and other anti-annexationists Riel agreed to a series of open negotiations with the Canadian representative, Donald Smith. A formal delegation was established by Riel's provisional government to negotiate with the Canadians and the provisional government was authorized to administer the settlement.

Negotiations between Riel's provisional government and the Canadian government proceeded during the first months of 1870. Eventually the Parliament of Canada enacted legislation granting provincial status to the newly established Province of Manitoba and establishing the rights demanded by Riel's provisional government. Riel continued to discuss possible annexation publicly. In actuality he had accepted involvement in the Canadian Confederation.

It is difficult to determine the real intentions of a Fenian leader such as O'Donaghue and his possible attempts at relating this Red River Rebellion to the overall efforts of the Fenian Brotherhood. The January 1, 1870, *Sioux City Weekly Times* published a dispatch from the Fenian circle of Leavenworth, Kansas. It implored Fenians of the region to seize the opportunity presented to find justice and revenge. The dispatch demanded revenge for Cromwell and Ireton's actions, and invoked the memories of Emmet, Fitzgerald, Wolfe Tone, and recent martyrs, Allen, Larkin, and O'Brien. It called for assistance to the native inhabitants of British North America who were in arms for independence. Such a blow against British North America was an indirect blow against England. The dispatch again stated that "England's difficulty is Ireland's opportunity".

The question of involvement in Fenian activities became a religious question for Irish Catholics when on January 12, 1870, Pope Pius IX, in a formal decree, declared that Fenianism, whether American or Hibernian (in Ireland), was included in the societies forbidden and condemned in the constitution of the supreme pontiff. Charley Collins in the *Sioux City Daily Times* of March 5, 1870, condemned the Pope's actions. A few days later he noted that there had been bold opposition by the Catholic clergy of both Ireland and America against the papal decree. Why were the Fenians condemned by the Catholic Church? The *Dakota Catholic* of July 6, 1889, gave this explanation. These societies "were condemned because an unlawful object was often veiled under pretexts of social and civil good, and these organizations pledged their members to absolute secrecy in many cases, to blind obedience in carrying out the dictates of their leaders" ...All societies...that "lead men into error and sin, are forbidden by the 'law of God'". [12]

The papal condemnation did not slow down Fenian activity in Sioux City. The Fenian Brotherhood of Sioux City held a grand ball on February 7, 1870, in order to raise money for the planned military activities. Members of the local circle included James P. Wall, Dennis O'Flaherty, Patrick R. Kennedy, John Burns, Patrick Daly, Patrick Walpole, Peter Johnson, Thomas E. Coleman, Michael Hogan, William O. Sparks, P.F. Sullivan, Al E. Caldwell, John Fitzgibbon, Edward Malone, and William S. Rollis. The gala event was attended by 153 couples and included thirty-six dances. John Brennan was called on by the members of the Circle to make a few remarks on the subject of Fenianism and to explain its intentions to the people present. He concluded his presentation with a patriotic poem by Michael Scanlan. Money was also raised to send a banner to the St. Patrick's Day Parade in Chicago using the Wolf Tone Circle's name.

The *Daily Times* gave frequent accounts of Fenian meetings in the east. The April 18th and 19th dispatches included mention of attempts at completing the Red River expedition and reports of arms shipments from Chicago to the Red River country. On May 20, 1870, the Daily Times reported that a large body of Fenian soldiers had arrived in Duluth en route to aid Riel. They were said to be under the direction of a former Confederate general and intended to capture Fort Francis or Rainy Lake. Another party was said to have started over the Vermillion Road, and another was to travel by canoes along the St. Louis and Vermillion Rivers. These activities were to part of the overall Fenian operation. These events are undocumented and may have been the figment of someone's imagination, maybe planned but never carried out. There is no additional documentation of these events. The May 25,1870 dispatch suggested that Fenian actions in the east were but diversions for the main activities in the Red River Valley. It also stated that the Red River Expedition had been approved by the entire Brotherhood organization.

It is a fact, however, that on May 25, 1870, John O'Neill led a second Fenian expedition toward the Canadian border. Two of the people involved in the second expedition were John Boyle O'Reilly and Michael Quinn. At this same time, President Ulysses Grant issued a proclamation against any infraction of the United States neutrality laws. O'Neill, along with several of the Fenian officers, were arrested and jailed. O'Neill was convicted of violation of the Neutrality Laws and spent three months in jail before he was released. O'Neill was an honored Union Civil War veteran, who had received permanent injuries as a result of his heroic acts.

The *Daily Times* suggested that O'Neill actions were not approved by a General Gleason and the Savage branch of the the Fenian Brotherhood. In fact, the Fenian Senate and O'Neill had split over the failure to carry out another invasion. By the spring of 1870, the funds being contributed to the Fenian organization had decreased considerably. On May 30, 1870, the Wolfe Tone Circle of Sioux City met to raise money for the "men in the front". Several of the speakers stated that they were opposed to General O'Neill's actions outside the Fenian organization but because the men were in the field they believed that they should be supported. $323.50 was raised. Making subscriptions and pledges were: Pat Rollis, James P. Vail, Tim Mulligan, P.R. Kennedy, Tim McCarty, John Hickey, William Cody, Michael Hogan, John Dineen, H A. Smith, Patrick Walpole, Pat Allan, John Fitzgibbon, James Irwin, William F. and Mrs. Follis, John Donovan, Peter Johnson, Michael O'Keefe, Bartholmew Crowley, Robert McKena, Patrick Hayes, Stephen Coleman, Edmund Regan, John Brennan, Daniel Hartnett, John Dagner, Michael Healy, Pat Donnelly, F.M. MacDonagh, Daniel Dermody, John Ryan, Patrick Gosson, Tim Sullivan, B.D. Kathrens, Pat Daly, John McAlister, John Fisher, Thomas Hopkins, Harry Gilmore, John McQuillan, John Roach, Martin and Mrs. Hinchy, John McCartney, James Maloney, George Schuster, Henry I. Brown, Dan Flynn, James McKenna, and J.A. McGee.

Fenian meetings in Sioux City were held throughout the summer of 1870. Eventually news of O'Neill's capture reached the Wolf Tone Circle. Apparently local support for the military actions waned. Charles Collins, in the August 11, 1870 *Daily Times,* made this editorial comment:

"By reference to our report of the Irish national meeting, it will be seen that our Irish citizens are alive to the necessity for withholding their sympathies for either beligerants abroad, until it can be seen in which direction England will be drawn by the growing complications.

This is sense and business combined. Let Poor Canada alone, and if blows are to struck at the tyrant of the Isle, let them aim at her vitals and be given simultaneously with those from stronger and more experienced hands.

The recent manifestations of interest in Napoleon by hot-headed enthusiasts at the east, were in extremely bad taste, but may now be corrected in time to avert mishaps similar to the result of previous Fenian movements in this country."

The August 26 *Daily Times* reported that the Irish National Brotherhood, or the United Irishmen had been organized as a successor to Fenianism. By November 29, 1870, the Wolfe Tone Circle would begin to reorganize and become a branch of the United Irishmen. By May 4, 1871, the Fenian Hall in Sioux City had become an office and the money dispersed amongst its members.

To the north, W.B. O'Donaghue continued his efforts for the Fenian cause. O'Donaghue and Enos Stutsman did succeed in getting a memorial passed by the Metis provisional government to propose to the United States the possibility of annexing the Metis lands. O'Donaghue, in the fall of 1870, traveled to Washington, D.C. to present the proposal to President Grant.

The *St. Paul Weekly Press* of October 27, 1870, reported that O'Donaghue had arrived in St. Paul on his way to Washington, with the memorial. The article stated that after the initial resistance by the Provisional Government, the Canadian government had offered complete amnesty to the members of the provisional government if they would accept the Manitoba Act establishing Canadian jurisdiction over their land. The act offered creation of a new province, certain guaranteed rights and land titles, a legislature, and a voice in the newly organized Dominion of Canada. The Metis provisional government, after mediation, accepted the offer. A large Canadian force was allowed to pass through American territory, after reassurances of complete amnesty to the United State government, and enter Rupert's Land unopposed. The force proceeded to Fort Garry where they arrested every Riel supporter they could apprehend. The Canadian military also threatened to kill any provisional government leader they could catch before they were expelled from the territory. This occurred in spite of the fact that Louis Riel considered himself and his followers loyal subjects of the Queen of England. Riel and fellow Metis leader, Ambroise Lepine fled to St. Joseph's, west of Pembina. W.B. O'Donaghue moved to Pembina.

The Metis leaders, upset with the Canadian government actions met in St. Norbert's on September 17, 1870. They authorized O'Donaghue to carry a memorial to United States President Ulysses

Grant asking that he use his office to ensure that all of the Metis grievances against the Canadian government be remedied. The Metis council refused to include a request for American annexation proposed by O'Donaghue. Apparently Riel and O'Donaghue had a major quarrel over the contents of the memorial. O'Donaghue decided to carry out his activities on his own. Without consulting the Metis leaders O'Donaghue went to Enos Stutsman. Stutsman and O'Donaghue decided to include a request for annexation without telling the Metis leaders. After consultation with Roman Catholic Bishop Tache, Riel chose to return to Manitoba and continue to negotiate with the Canadians.

The Irish of the community would underestimate the amount of determination the Metis had in their attempt at obtaining their complete independence from the Canadian government. O'Donaghue traveled to Washington D.C. in December, 1870. He met and was eventually assisted by Senator Alexander Ramsey of Minnesota, General N. P. Banks, chairman of the committee on foreign relations in the U.S. House of Representatives, and Senator Zachariah Chandler of Michigan. Senator Ramsey secured an audience for O'Donaghue with U.S. President Grant on January 29, 1871. After the ensuing discussion, President Grant decided not to give support to O'Donaghue's activities and to the memorial proposed by Riel's provisional government. During O'Donaghue's travels to the eastern United States he met with financier, Jay Cooke in New York in February, 1871. At a later meeting in Philadelphia in March, O'Donaghue attempted to persuade Cooke to become involved in the annexation plans in Rupert's Land. Cooke informed O'Donaghue that he could not become involved for fear of jeopardizing his business interests in England.[13]

Apparently some time in late 1870 or during the first months of 1871, W.B. O'Donaghue made contact with John O'Neill. O'Donaghue met with the Fenian Council, who refused to have anything to do with activities in Manitoba. Apparently he convinced O'Neill to become involved, however. Later court testimony from residents of St. Paul, Minnesota stated that John O'Neill spent time in the first months of 1871 in St. Paul attempting to solicit funds to create an Irish colony in Dakota Territory, near the U.S.-Canadian border.

During the summer of 1871, a considerable number of Irish men appeared and camped on the military reservation at Fort Sully. South Dakota historian, Doane Robinson believed that Charley Collins was involved in the supplying of Fenian soldiers at his settlement at Brule City, Dakota Territory. [19] His statements of the previous fall tend to contradict this conclusion. General Stanley, the post commander at Fort Sully, an Irish Catholic, found out what the purpose of the Irish men gathering on the military reserve was. He ordered them off of the military reservation. The group was seen at Fort Yates and the commander there forced them off.

A military report by United States Army Captain Loyd Wheaton, commander of Fort Pembina, Dakota Territory, detailed the activities of the Fenians in the fall of 1871.[14] Captain Wheaton reported that half-breeds were harvesting large quantities of hay near St. Joseph, Dakota Territory. The operation was financed by money from Fenians. Wheaton stated that a half-breed by the name of Poitras had harvested 50 tons of hay for his employer, Doyle, who resided at St. Joseph. It was reported that O'Donoghue crossed the Red River at Georgetown, Minnesota with four wagons containing about 40 men. They were last seen crossing the Tongue River and disappearing in the direction of St. Joseph, Dakota Territory. On the 29th of September, O'Donaghue arrived in Pembina at the same time "small bodies" of unarmed men crossed the Park, or Little Salt River in the direction of Pembina. An officer sent by Wheaton to the Pembina Mountains, 30 miles west of Pembina, reported that O'Neill, Curley, and Donelly were observed addressing each other by the titles of "General" and "Colonel". O'Donaghue was seen with O'Neill, Curley, and Donelly at the home of a Mr. Grant. They were headed to the home of Doyle at St. Joseph on the night of the 4th of October. Wheaton ordered Lieutenant Charles O'Bradley and a detachment of mounted infantry to apprehend the force.

On the 5th of October, a body of men armed with muskets and marching in columns of fours crossed the international border in the direction of the Dominion Custom House at Pembina. They were led by O'Donaghue on horseback. O'Neill, armed with a sword, Curley, and Donelly served as officers. The Custom House was seized in the name of the Provisional Government of Rupert's Land. The Hudson's Bay Company's Trading Post was occupied and the stores of the Company were removed. Muskets, cartridges, and sabres were brought in. Horses and wagons were seized.

The Fenians were operating with a survey map completed in 1823. Captain Wheaton possessed the survey of the international boundary completed the summer of 1870 by Captain D.P. Heap of the U.S. Army Corps of Engineers. As a result, Wheaton loaded his 20th Infantry detachment into wagons and advanced to within 1000 yards of the Hudson's Bay Post. They destroyed a line of skirmishes during the advance. The Fenian's map indicated that the Custom House was in Canadian territory. The new survey placed the Custom House in American territory. Captain Wheaton then captured O'Neill, Curley, Donelly and ten men. Ninety-four muskets, eleven sabres, and 12,000 cartridges were seized.

Wheaton reported that W.B. O'Donaghue had been captured by a half-breed, and was turned over by the Hudson's Bay authorities to Lieutenant John Bannister of the 20th Infantry. O'Neill, Curley, Donelly, and O'Donaghue were turned over to U.S. Commissioner Foster at Pembina, Dakota Territory. Wheaton estimated the number of men under arms to be between from 40 to 80. He also noted that a number of residents of the town of Pembina and vicinity were in the Fenian organization. The greater number were "persons apparently of Irish descent and strangers to this vicinity".[15]

There was no organized support given the Fenians by the Metis under Louis Riel. By this time, the Metis once again considered themselves loyal members of the British Empire. Enos Stutsman had given up any hope of annexation of Rupert's Land by the United States.

Wheaton, in his report, commented that he hoped that O'Neill, O'Donaghue, Donelly, and Curley would not be released by the civil authorities. He believed that the "lawless characters inhabiting the town of Pembina" might attempt further actions if their release did occur.

Hired to represent the Fenian leaders were co-counsels, George Potter and Enos Stutsman. Interestingly, Stutsman owned the building that housed the Pembina courtroom and jail. When Winnipeg lawyer J.F. Bain appeared in the court to request the extradition of W.B. O'Donaghue to Canada, he found that the prisoner, O'Donaghue, had been released. The *St. Paul Weekly Press*' account stated that Commissioner Foster had determined that the Dominion Custom House had been, in fact, in Canadian territory. He ruled that the capture had therefore been improper. All of the leaders were released.

O'Neill and Curley were later arrested by the United States Marshall in Minnesota. In a letter to the U.S. Attorney General on January 28, 1872, Attorney General for Dakota Territory, Warren Cowles, stated that "these reckless and misguided men" should be prosecuted and convicted in "a brief, easy, and certain affair". After further observations, Cowles decided not to prosecute the group. He believed that the travel, expenses, and the inability to find a jury in Pembina willing to convict the group, did not warrant the prosecution.

In thirteen cases that Cowles had prosecuted all of the defendants, including William Barry, had been acquitted by Dakota Territory juries. This situation of apparent lawlessness would lead to the appointment of Peter Shannon, an Irish Catholic, as the Chief Justice of the Dakota Territory Supreme Court in 1873. It also increased the importance of the need to successfully prosecute Jack McCall for the murder of "Wild" Bill Hickok in 1876.

Charles Collins, in his 1879 directory, stated that W.B. O'Donaghue, leading John O'Neill on the ill-fated raid on Pembina, created a major split among the American Fenians.[16]

In such a situation it is difficult to determine the extent of the Fenian operation in the region. Apparently, Michael Quinn, a participant in the second excursion, was located to the south as part of a support group. He would later state that he traveled to Colorado with the leader of this Fenian group, after the collapse of the "Capture Canada" campaign. Michael's travels would include further involvement in Irish settlement in the region.[17]

Testimony at the Federal Court hearing in St. Paul indicated that logistical, financial, and material support was received from the Irish American community of St. Paul.

Years later an arms store was found in the Lincoln, Nebraska basement of the late Irish American businessman and politician, John Fitzgerald. The arms had been originally stored in the Nebraska State Capitol building. Apparently, they had been left over from the Civil War. Irishmen in Lincoln asked then Governor Butler to contribute the store to the Riel Rebellion taking place in Manitoba. Butler refused to make a public contribution but did agree to overlook the disappearance of the arms if his name would remain anonymous. Eventually, the breechloaders were shipped to Minnesota. After the collapse of the third excursion John Fitzgerald paid the freight to return the arms to Lincoln. Apparently Fitzgerald held on to the arms in case they were to be used in future actions. One of the breechloaders is currently in the collection of the Nebraska State Museum in Lincoln. The arms were rediscovered upon Fitzgerald's death.[18]

Also uncovered in a metal box in the Fitzgerald residence were a roster of the Fenian army and the index of the Fenian organization, including a description of the "head-center" in New York. The index supposedly included a list of over 200,000 ex-Civil War soldiers. Whereabouts of these papers is at the present time not known. What were W.B. O'Donaghue's intentions in leading the operation to Rupert's Land in October of 1871? Why would he do so without the support of Riel and the Metis or the Fenian General Council? Did he even consider the effects of the weather on military activities this far north during the winter months? Did he carry out the activities hoping that a Canadian force could not reach the region until spring? O'Donaghue, after his release, was taken in by Jim Callan, an Irish farmer, who lived a few miles south of St. Paul in Dakota County, Minnesota. He eventually obtained a job as a rural school teacher.[19]

After this third failed attempt at attacking Britain through Canada, O'Neill turned his efforts to the formation of a colonization effort in Nebraska. As his speeches indicate, he did not completely swear off further military actions against Canada.

The Metis would eventually accept their role within the Dominion of Canada. Louis Riel would later be executed by the Canadian authorities.

Changes in politics back in Ireland and among the Irish Nationalists in America eventually led to the decline of the Fenian movement by the late 1870s. William W. Roberts, a wealthy New York merchant, was elected to the U. S. House of Representatives in 1870 and 1872. The Irish of the region would now concentrate their efforts on colonization.

1   Desmond Ryan, edited by T. M. Moody, "O'Mahony", The Fenian Movement (Mercier Press, Dublin and Cork, 1968, 1978), Pages 63-75.

2   History of the St. Simon and Jude Parish, Flandreau, Flandreau File, Diocese of Sioux Falls Archives.

3   Fargo Forum, (North Dakota), May 2, 1914.

4   Richard Droda, Irish Colonization In Nebraska, O'Neill and Greeley, (Nebraska State Historical Society, Lincoln, 1936), Pages 1-12., Sister Mary Martin Langan, O.P., General John O'Neill Soldier, and Leader of Irish Catholic Colonization in America, (Notre Dame University, Notre Dame, Indiana, 1937), Pages 11-24.

5   Doane Robinson, "Fenians in Dakota", South Dakota Historical Collections, 1912 (Pierre, 1912), Pages 117-130b; Doane Robinson, "Fenians in South Dakota", Dictionary of South Dakota (South Dakota Historical Society, Pierre, 1925), Pages 224-225.

6   Homer Calkins, "The Irish In Iowa", The Palimpsest, Volume XLV, No.2, (Iowa City, Iowa, 1964), Pages 33-55.

7   Henry Casper, S. J., The History of the Catholic Church In Nebraska (Bruce Press, Milwaukee, 1960), Pages 99-116.

8   Sioux City Times, November 11, 1870.

9   Gerald Mattson, Church On The Seven Mile Prairie, St. Joseph Parish, Farmington, Minnesota (Farmington, Minnesota, 1982), Pages 197-199, 269.

10   Elwyn B. Robinson, History of North Dakota (University of Nebraska Press, 1966), Pages 110-112.

11   Dale Gibson, Attorney For the Frontier, Enos Stutsman, (University of Manitoba Press, 1983), Pages 97-147.

12   Dakota Catholic, July 6, 1889, Page 3.

13   John Perry Pritchett, editor, "Letter from W.B. O'Donaghue to Jay Cooke, March 29, 1871", Anent the O'Donaghue Scheme for the Annexation of Rupert's Land, North Dakota Historical Quarterly, Volume V, No.1, 1930, Pages 49-51.

14   Record Group No. 94, Records of the Adjutant General's Office, 1780s-1917, Letters received, #3542 (1871), filed with 3248 (1871), (National Archives, Washington, D.C.)

15   Doane Robinson, "Fenians In Dakota", South Dakota

Historical Collections, 1912, (Pierre, South Dakota, 1912), Pages 117-127.

16   Charles Collins, Black Hills History and Directory for 1878-79 (Sioux City, Iowa, 1879), Page 4.

17   Interview with Michael Quinn, Rapid City, (S.D.) Journal, no date.

18   James Manahan, Trials of A Lawyer, Autobiography by James Manahan, (St. Paul, 1933), Pages 13-31.

19   Gerald Mattson, Church On The Seven Mile Prairie, St. Joseph Parish, Farmington, Minnesota,(Farmington, Minnesota, 1982), Pages 197-199.

CHAPTER 3

THE IRISH IMMIGRATION
CONVENTION: VERMILLION, 1872

The Irish of the region would now concentrate their efforts on colonization. On September 18, 1872, a letter from John Brennan appeared in the *Sioux City Journal*.

"Will we do it? If yes let us attend the Vermillion Convention. If not let us cease to babble about patriotism and fraternal love."

"The convention, from assurances that we have received, promises to be the most thoroughly representative Irish gathering that has ever been assemble in the West, as large delegations will be present from every organized county in South Dakota and Northeastern Nebraska."

" All persons of this city and county who intend to attend the convention, are requested to meet at the Times office at 1 o'clock today, Wed., to make arrangements to go in a body.

By order of the committee."

John Brennan, Sec.

The *Sioux City Journal*, the same day, printed the following announcement:[1]

IRISH IMMIGRATION CONVENTION

Since the call for the convention was issued three weeks ago, we have received communication from O'Donavan Rossa, Michael Scanlan, and other distinguished Irishmen, wishing the work God's speed, and pledging it their sympathy and support.

Join with us in the initiation of this grand move for the social regeneration of our people. We ask

them to see to it that our brethren receive their
share of the public domain or all the best land is
held in other hands. Two roads lie before Irish
people in America, the one, the straight, broad,
long one runs Westward and leads to virtue,
dignity, independence, and a home. The other
winds through the crowed cities of the East and is
the track over which travel the historical "hewers
of wood and drawers of water." To guide them over
the straight road is our duty and is in our hands."

This appears to be the work of John Brennan.

George Kingsbury's History of South Dakota credits John
Stanage with the chairmanship of the convention. However, the
Vermillion Dakota Republican of September 26, 1870, stated that
John Brennan of Sioux City was chosen President, James McHenry
of Vermillion became the Vice-President, and Charles Collins, of the
Sioux City Times, and T.F. Singiser of the *Yankton Herald* were the
secretaries.

The Convention produced two resolutions which appeared in
Kingsbury's History. The Committee on Resolutions produced the
following statement:

"Whereas it has pleased God that the pressure
of bad government, and the force of circumstances,
and of choice, has transplanted one half of the Irish
race from their own soil to this free land;

"And whereas, many of our brother Irishmen,
through poverty, negligence, and apathy have
located in the densely populated districts of the
East, where if they remain, many of them must
remain poor, indigent, and subject to the
contaminating influences of city life.

"And whereas, Our experience has taught us
that life in the West is conducive to the
independence, wealth, dignity, health, honor, and
purity of Irish men and their families wherefore, be
it resolved:

"First, that we earnestly invite and beseech our people in Ireland, Canada and the East to seek new homes in this free, independent, healthy, and productive land;

"Second, that we appeal to our wealthy, powerful, and educated countrymen in the East to foster, promote and encourage Irish immigration to the Northwest;

"Third, that we, the Irish-American and cosmopolitan citizens of this convention, pledge our experience, sympathy, and aid to such of them as may come."

The Committee on Experience and Addresses produced the following resolution:

"We, the Committee on Experience and Address, recommend that the chairman and upon the citizens of this convention, residents of the Northwest, to write their individual experience in the West, and place it in comparison with the East, and that such experience be published for the information of emigrants."

Appointed to carry out this activity were:

James McHenry, Vermillion; C.D. Owens, Clay Co. Dakota; Judge Smith, Vermillion; T. J. Sloan, Vermillion, at the time serving as the Territorial Treasurer; T.F. Singiser, Yankton; L. McCarthy, Sioux City; Michael Ryan, Barney Mohan, Alick Keevil, Mike Curry, all farmers of Union County, Dakota.

At the beginning of the twentieth century, Kingsbury noted that the result of the subsequent efforts made by the members of this convention could be told by the Irish American citizens who have in goodly numbers, since made their homes in Dakota.[2] Kingsbury was correct in his conclusion that Irish immigration to Dakota did increase in the years immediately after the Vermillion Convention of 1872. The drought years of the early 1870s discouraged many farmers from settling in Dakota. The Panic of 1873 would force other immigrants to seek a better situation on the farm lands of eastern Dakota. The Irish would also play an important role in the gold rush to the Black Hills of Dakota.

Irish people established several, initial settlements in Dakota during this period. The Bon Homme settlement included several Irish settlers.[3] [14] Bridget Cogan, a Roman Catholic native of County Roscommon, Ireland, and the widowed mother of a young son, A.J. Cogan, came to live with her brother, Barney Cole, the blacksmith of Bon Homme, in 1869. Bridget and Barney built a large structure that was to be used as a hotel. Soon after its completion, the wooden building burnt down. Bridget moved into the building that served as the courthouse and operated the structure as a hotel when the U.S. District Court was not in session. Bridget housed all of the judges, lawyers, and business people who visited the District Court. She also baked all of the bread and cooked all of the meals. The Native American people who visited the area called her the "big white woman who keeps the eating house". In the spring of 1876 Bridget Cogan's hotel housed General George Custer and the Seventh Cavalry. They were detained for several days due to high water. Custer entered the local residents by putting on displays of his shooting ability from the porch of the hotel. During their stay

Bridget Cogan, prominent
resident of the Bon Homme
Settlement. Kingsbury's
History of Dakota Territory.

at Bon Homme, the troops were stricken with a virus which caused the death of several troopers. Six Irish American soldiers from the Seventh Cavalry are buried in the Bon Homme Cemetery. Listed among the six are Crowley, J. Delaney and A. Hirsh.

Peter Byrne, an Irish born Catholic, came from Dubuque to Yankton, Dakota Territory in 1869. He moved to Bon Homme in 1870. He filled a pre-emption claim near Bon Homme and a timber claim east of Tyndall. His first employment in the area was rafting cottonwood across the Missouri River at Yankton for George Kingsbury. He constructed a saw mill at Bon Homme. In 1874, Peter married Ann Lindley, a native of England and a member of the Congregational Church. He remained a Catholic. His land holdings in the area grew to more than two thousand acres in Dakota and three thousand acres in Montana. He eventually moved into Tyndall where he became vice-president of the Security State Bank.

In 1879, Mrs. Mary Dwyer, the widow of Patrick Dwyer donated five acres of land to Bishop Martin Marty. The land was located one half mile east, three miles south, and one half mile east of where Tyndall was eventually located. It was to be used for the location of

Cogan House, Bon Homme, Dakota Territory. Courtesy of the South Dakota Historical Society.

a cemetery, church, and parish house. This was the location of the Sacred Heart Settlement in which Father Meinrad McCarthy resided.

In 1871, John Michael Crowley, T.J. and Thomas Crowley, James, Patrick and Will Hurley, Irish born, Cornelius Collins, Thomas Quigley, Michael Harney, John Brazzel, and Frank Leahy settled in the area which became Lincoln County and later the town of Lennox.[4] [20] In 1871, C.W. Norton settled on a homestead three miles east of present day Worthing.

In 1872, the James Madden and the Phillip and Maria Madden Devitt family homesteaded in an area a short distance from the Sioux River south and west of Sioux Falls. James Madden's homestead later developed into the town of Worthing. [21] The homestead boundaries were uncharacteristically longer and narrower than the usual 160 acres square. Because 1872 was a very dry year, only one edge of the homestead area contained any prairie grass. That portion was divided equally into three equal portions. George Clark and his wife Kate Madden Clark arrived in the Worthing area from Springfield in 1876.

James Madden, organizer of the Worthing settlement. 100 Years, Worthing, South Dakota.

Father Christian Knauf, land agent and pastor for the Catholic Colonization Bureau colony in Adrian, Minnesota, provided Lennox, Sioux Falls, and Dell Rapids Catholics with opportunities to practice their religion. Most of the Irish settlers were Roman Catholic. In 1877, Father Knauf organized the Saint Augustine Society in Lennox. The Society was responsible for the eventual construction of the Catholic church in Lennox.[5] In 1878, Irish families moved from the Caledonia settlement of Houston County, Minnesota into the area which became the town of Elkton. The homesteads were concentrated in Parnell and Alton Townships.

In 1871 John O'Grady and John McClellan were joined in the Sioux Falls settlement by Irish born, John McKee. He lived in a

Left to right; Kate Madden Clark, Maria Madden Devitt, and Phillip H. Devitt of the Worthing settlement. Courtesy of Marian Devitt.

dugout during his first year on his claim. John Powers, his father and his brother, Allen, all Irish born arrived in Minnehaha in 1873. Another brother, Owen arrived in 1874. Patrick Gallagher began a successful farming operation in Minnehaha County in 1875.[6]

The Irish population of Sioux Falls grew steadily. P.P. Boylan arrived in 1877, J.M. Murray in 1878, Mike Gerin in January, 1879, H.H. Carroll in 1881. All were Irish born. Another Irish born arrival to Sioux Falls in September, 1879 was Daniel O'Donaghue. Daniel, born in County Wexford in 1831, had taken his family from Ireland to Ontario, Canada, during the potato famine of the 1840s. He learned the brickmaking trade while in Canada. He and his family migrated to Chicago and eventually to Decorah, Iowa. While in Decorah, Daniel left his family and took two of his sons, probably Stephen and John H., and joined O'Neill's group who "were heading to California to the Gold Rush." They traveled as far as Omaha. They traveled to O'Neill, Nebraska and then to Marysville, Kansas. In Marysville they created the bricks for the Catholic Church. After two years in Kansas, Daniel brought his family to Sioux Falls in 1878. Immediately after his arrival in Sioux Falls, he changed his family name to Donahoe. The oral tradition of his family is that they left O'Neill because the Fenians were fighting amongst each other.

Father Christian Knauf, pastor and land agent of the Catholic Colonization Bureau. Courtesy of the Archives of the Archdiocese of St. Paul and Minneapolis.

The author has not established the possible connection between Daniel and William B. O'Donaghue. William was born in the northwestern part of Ireland. Daniel was born in the south of Ireland.[7] Daniel's son, John, married Julia Barnett, daughter of George Barnett. George Barnett moved to Sioux Falls from the Catholic Colonization Bureau colony in Adrian, Minnesota.

On May 9, 1879, Father C.J. Knauf purchased property in the West Sioux Falls addition.[8] This was land which had been platted by John McClellan, by this time a real estate agent, who resided at 6th Street and Minnesota Avenue. P.P. Boylan and J.M. Murray were the first two lay incorporators of Saint Michael's Church. Daniel Donahoe provided the brick for the second church structure built in 1883. The first structure, made of wood, was destroyed by a prairie fire in 1881.

Minnehaha County's Irish population increased during the this period. Edward and Michael Flynn, Humphrey Murphy, and Timothy O'Connell homesteaded in the western portion of the county. Sylvester Delaney was located in the same area. James and John Gilmore, and Patrick McAvary located in Clear Lake Township between 1878 and 1881. John Murray, Marshall McConnell, Tom McGinity, Mike Riley and James Treacy located in Wall Lake Township. Irish born, Patrick Gallagher established a large cattle operation north of Wall Lake. William Kelly located near Lyons in 1874. Irish born Owen and Tom McBride came to the county in 1874.[9] An 1882 Dakota Territory map shows a Celton community in the southwest corner of Minnehaha County. [23]

Irish settlers from Goodhue County, Minnesota, established the Montrose settlement in 1878.[10] [61] Settlers included members of the McDowell, Calleran, Lally, Murphy, Enright, Sullivan, McAllovy, Wheeler, Kelly, Narney, O'Kelley, and Mulloy families. The first Catholic mass was conducted in the Lally home on St. Patrick's Day, 1879. Father Ahern, who established a mission at the settlement, considered calling it Clontarf. Montrose was platted in 1879.

The Bridgewater settlement included members of the McNaboe, Quinn, Kelly, McCarthy, Riley, Nugent, O'Rourke, Farley, Fitzgerald, Kappenman, Baldwin, Jennings, Shelly, O'Gara,

O'Brien, and Ryan families. The town of Bridgewater was platted in 1881. [48]

Yankton's Irish population increased as well. Irish born Owen Bartlett was the local liquor dealer until 1870.[11] E.C. Dudley came to Yankton in 1869, and established a hardware store. The first recorded baptism was of a child of hardware owner, James Donahoe in 1871.[12] The police force of Yankton consisted of one officer, Sheriff P.C. Conway. At one time Conway was dismissed for selling liquor to the city jail inmates. He did so in order to make more money. He did not receive a salary and was paid two dollars an arrest. He was rehired when a replacement was not found.[13] In December, 1872, Conway began rounding up the town's prostitutes. Each person was fined from five to ten dollars in the justice court. As a result, Conway soon received a living wage.

Peter C. Shannon became a judge in Pennsylvania at the age of twenty-eight. He served as state representative from Pittsburg. He

The second St. Michael's Church, Sioux Falls, 1882. Located on present site of St. Joseph's Cathedral. Built with bricks from the Donahoe's Brickyard. Courtesy of the Archives of the Diocese of Sioux Falls.

served in the Union Army during the Civil War. He turned down several political appointments by Abraham Lincoln, but eventually accepted Ulysses Grant's appointment as the chief justice of the supreme court of Dakota Territory in March, 1873. He helped organize the court system for the Pembina district. Judge Peter C. Shannon was sent to Yankton, Dakota Territory, in 1874 in order to attempt to improve the criminal justice system. Shannon, an Irish Catholic, succeeded in establishing the power of the judiciary in the Territory. Shannon became the leader in the Territorial judiciary after his appointment as chief justice. The Territorial courts came to be called Shannon's court. The conviction and resulting execution of Jack McCall was one of Peter Shannon's first judicial decisions. He retired from the court in January, 1883. He served on the Sioux Indian Land Commission during his retirement.[14] Peter also became a leader of the Catholic Church in Yankton. At the time of his accidental death in 1899 he was creating a history of the early Catholic Church in the region. His official papers were not preserved.

In 1875, Yankton Catholics, Joseph Pier, J.N. Hatert, John McNamara, Robert O'Neill, James Griffin and John Walsh purchased land for a second Catholic church.[15] It was completed within the year. Yankton city aldermen included W.M. Powers and Patrick Brennan. James, and Irish born Michael, Brennan operated a market. Michael married Kate Walsh in Yankton in 1877.[16] R.G. Grady served as the tailor. M.M. Sullivan was employed as a musician. The Yankton Irish community contributed to the Irish National League.

Irish born Mike Griffin's residence in Springfield was the location, in 1872, of the first Catholic marriage in the town. Griffin would serve for a long period as the town's postmaster.

J. H. Gallagher and William Dwyer were among the settlers in Turner County in 1873. John Rooth donated land for a Catholic Church which was built in 1874. The church was the first Catholic Church in Turner County.17 [44]

In 1879, M.H. Day, who, along with Charles Collins, had established the Brule City town site, located in the Turner County settlement of Swan Lake. [24] He was soon after elected Turner County's representative to the Dakota Territorial Legislature. The Catholic Church at Swan Lake was located two and one half miles south, and two miles west of present day Hurley.[18] The church at Swan Lake was eventually closed and sold off. St. Joachim's Church in Hurley was built during 1884-85. It was dedicated in August 19, 1886.

In 1874, Michael O'Shea became the trader at the Running Water trading post. O'Shea had mustered out of Fort Randall. This settlement eventually became to be called the Running Water Irish Settlement.[19] [16]

In 1877, Irish families, including the Devaneys, Keneficks, Collins, Caseys, Clancys, Naughtons, Finnegans, Meads, and Driscolls settled nine to sixteen miles north and west of Dell Rapids. The St. Michael's parish in Moody County developed from this community. [38]

The military population of the Fort Randall was an exception to the general pattern of settlement in the region. [2] As previously noted, from the first years, the military population and their dependents were at many times predominantly Irish. Several Irish American soldiers would later muster out of the army and become the first settlers in the region. Like the population at any military installation, it could change dramatically with just the movement of one military battalion to another military post.

The Twenty-second Infantry was first stationed at Fort Randall in January of 1867. During the summer of 1871, the stage line from Yankton was established. This allowed the post's baseball team, the O'Reilly's, to travel to Yankton to take on the Yankton Coyote Ball Club.[20] During the winter of 1872-73, the Irish population at Fort Randall formed an Irish Nationalism Organization among the troops of the Twenty-second Infantry. In May of 1873, the Catholic population started a newspaper owned by the St. Malochi's Roman Catholic Benevolent and Literary Association. It was edited by James Day and Hugh McDonald. The Catholic congregation established a church in an old, empty building. During the summer of 1874, the Twenty-second Infantry was transferred to the Military Division of the Atlantic. They would return to the region as part of

General Terry's Little Big Horn Campaign of 1876. In 1875, a chalk rock chapel was constructed and dedicated as a church for all denominations. It was used as the location for various religious celebrations. The original Fort Randall Catholic congregation eventually became part of the Catholic congregation which established the Saint Francis mission church. The Kirwan family that farms near the present day Fort Randall site, are descendants of Irish American Catholic people who homesteaded on the Fort Randall Military Reserve. The first Kirwan operated a farm that provided produce for the military population.[21]

Across from Fort Randall on the east side of the Missouri River, and within the boundaries of the Yankton Reservation, was the White Swan community. Located in the Clarkson's store was the telegraph office operated by an Irishman, J.R. Kilpatrick. This office was the western terminus of the telegraph line that ran through Yankton to Sioux City. All dispatches for the military posts on the upper Missouri River were received and forwarded from this office.

Charles Collins also continued his efforts at forming a settlement along the Missouri River, in spite of his party's initial difficulty with Jim Somers. Settlement was prohibited north of the Fort Randall Military Reserve by Presidential Addition in 1872. Collins platted out the settlement of Brule City on the east side of the Missouri River near the mouth of the White River.[22] [19] Brule City's first resident was Jim Somers. Somers was married to a Dakota woman. Estimated at nearly 6 feet 5 inches in height, he was described by some as the toughest man in the territory. Shortly before he took up residence at Brule City, Somers, Jack Sully, and William McKay were involved in the hanging of William Holbrough and Henry Hirl. That incident may have enhanced his image as the man to be reckoned with in the settlement. By the fall of 1873, D.W. Spaulding, with his wife and three children, J.R. Lowe, Fred Hemingway, D. Herman, E.C. Howard, and M.H. Day had established residence at Brule City. James McHenry transported a team powered saw mill to the site to provide lumber for the buildings of the new town site. Charles Collins transported a printing press to his claim. In the first issues of the Brule City Times

Collins described the town as having a boulevard two miles long. A coal vein was supposedly located within a few miles of the site. Collins did succeed in getting Peter Nelson, a real estate agent from Chicago, to bring thirteen families out from Illinois. They arrived in August of 1874. By October 13, a post office was opened.[23]

At this same time the Gordon-Russell party left Sioux City under the guise of heading to O'Neill's Colony in Nebraska and under the sponsorship of amongst others, Charles Collins. The party headed up the Niobrara River attempting to reach the Black Hills to the west. Of course, the Gordon-Russell party is quite famous for their role in confirming the fact that gold could be found in the Black Hills. Annie Tallent was the only female member of the party. Several authors have suggested that the reason Collins had located at the Brule City site was because it was the closest location to the Black Hills along the Missouri River. Collins perhaps believed that such a location would become the trading area to the east of the Hills. Although settlement in the area was still legally restricted by the United States government, the Dakota Territory Legislature organized the area around Brule City into Brule County. They appointed three county commissioners and named M.H. Day as the Register of Deeds. The U.S. military prevented further expeditions into the Black Hills during 1875. By the fall of 1875, only three of the fourteen original families from Illinois were still at the Brule City site. The post office closed in December, 1875. Activity returned to Brule City in March of 1876 when the Grant administration changed its policy and began to allow expeditions into the Black Hills. The trail through the Badlands to the Black Hills was to be used by the people seeking to find gold in the Hills. Six freighters who set out from Brule City in the spring of 1876 were killed by the Lakota at some location along the Badlands trail. That same year, Andrew Nelson, a Norwegian born carpenter, established a cattle ranch five miles from the Brule City site.

The U.S. Government officially opened the Black Hills for settlement in the spring of 1877. The Dakota Territorial Legislature passed the Black Hills Wagon Road Act, authorizing three roads into the Black Hills. One was a route from Brule City to Deadwood. In spite of the the large amount of material transported into the Black Hills during the 1877 season, not one steamboat used the Brule City location to moor and unload its supplies.[24] Wagon trains used the route up the Niobrara River from Ft. Niobrara, or the trail that ran west from Fort Pierre, on the Missouri River, several miles north of the Brule City site. In 1879, the area around Brule City was finally legally opened for white settlement.

Charles Collins, while serving as Brule County Register of Deeds, established legal claim to the site. The claim included a detailed layout of the proposed Brule City town site. Obviously, Brule City did not become the "Fenian" colony described by some historians. It is quite impossible to determine Collins' exact intentions in promoting the establishment of the Brule City settlement.

By the spring of 1877, Collins had taken up residence in Deadwood. His printing equipment was destroyed by a fire on the Missouri River steamboat, Carroll. He was able to obtain another press and in June of 1877 he began to publish the *Black Hills Champion* as one of Deadwood's daily newspapers. In 1879, Collins released his book, Black Hills History and Directory.

During the summer of 1872, the *Sioux City Daily Times* printed articles "depicting the wonders of the Black Hills." The rumors of gold were also emphasized. Charles Collins exploits in encouraging illegal entry into the Black Hills have been described in detail by Annie Tallent and other participants in the early expeditions into the Black Hills.

John Brennan encouraged movement into the Hills with these lines of verse:

> In Dakota there are mountains
>> (and they're near Montana's line)
> Where Petroleum springs in fountain
>> And the hills are black with pine,
> An Oh, tis there the pioneer
>> His pouch with lure fills
> Black, stern, and bold, but rich in gold
>> Is the land of the "Black Hills."[25]

On October 5, 1874, the Gordon-Russell party left Sioux City for the Black Hills. Many of the people in the party had been civilian participants in General George Custer's expedition that established the fact that large quantities of gold were to found in the Black Hills. General Custer's expedition included several Irish Americans. Civilians, V.T. McGillicuddy and T.H. Mallory, and military officers, Kane, DeLany, and Bourke were among the many Irish American soldiers found in Custer's Seventh Cavalry force. The U.S. military policy was at this time was to deny access to the Hills to any white person.

The stated destination for the expedition was the newly established O'Neill Colony in northcentral Nebraska. [26] The party did eventually reach the Colony.[26] At this time the location consisted of no more than a few structures. Settlers did not arrive at the O'Neill Colony until over two years later. However, the party then proceeded to travel into the Black Hills, build a stockade, and winter in the Black Hills. It is difficult to determine by examining the names of the expedition participants whether any were Irish. Perhaps Thomas McLaren and Dan McDonald were Irish.

It can be stated that several Irish people were included in the first people to penetrate into the Black Hills at the time of the Gold Rush.[27] Irish born Paul Murphy, halted by troops in his first attempt into the Black Hills in the spring of 1875, eventually arrived in Custer in the fall of 1875. He established a saw mill that was later moved to Rockerville. During the fall of 1875, Ed Murphy was part of the expedition of miners from Montana that visited Deadwood Gulch. [27] This expedition was the first group to discover gold in Deadwood Gulch. Irish born John Manning came from Montana to Deadwood Gulch, arriving on March 16, 1876. He became the first elected sheriff of Lawrence County in 1877. Irish born Michael Heffron, a veteran of the Utah, California, Colorado, and Montana gold fields, arrived in Deadwood in April, 1876. He became involved in developing mining operations around Deadwood. Irish born James Lawler traveled from Yankton to Deadwood in March of 1876. He worked as a millwright and contractor along with his mining operations. Sam McMaster was born in Boardmills, County

Down, Ireland and was more than likely Scotch-Irish and not Irish. He was sent to the Black Hills in 1877 by California capitalists, Haggin, Tevis and George Hearst. They had formed the company that had purchased the Homestake mine in 1877. He served as the first superintendent of the Homestake mine. "Hookie Jack" Leary was one of the operators bought out when the Homestake mine was taken over by the California capitalists.

Fred T. Evans established the first freight line from Running Water and Pierre into the Black Hills in the spring of 1876.[28] William Doyle establish a lumber operation on Elk Creek, near Tilford prior to August, 1876. Felix Rooney was one of the leader of the miners who organized resistance to an attack by the Lakota on the miners in Deadwood Gulch in August of 1876. In the fall of 1876, a provisional government for Lawrence County was established by the people who had invaded the Hills. Among the officials of the government were Fred T. Evans and Joseph Flanner of the Crook City settlement, who was perhaps Irish. In several references, the Flanner name became Flannery, a recognizable Irish name. The government's first judge was J.M. Murphy. Richard W. Clark arrived at Crook City in April, 1876. He worked as a freight handler but is most famous for his impersonations of the fictional "Deadwood Dick" character in the Days of '76 celebrations. [33] Henry Frawley, just out of law school in Wisconsin, arrived in the Centennial Valley in 1877. He eventually established a legal practice in Deadwood, while ranching in the Centennial Valley.

A miner's union, organized as a result of perhaps. one of the first sitdown strikes in American labor history, was established in the northern Black Hills in the spring of 1877. The first president of the Union was Pat O'Grady. Irish American prospectors, along with their Welsh and Scottish counterparts, brought knowledge of hard rock mining techniques into the gold rush operations. Several had developed knowledge of these techniques while prospecting in Montana, Colorado, and California.

Two associates of Buffalo Bill Cody were Irish born residents of the Black Hills. Michael Russell served as buffalo hunter with Cody in Kansas. He came to the Hills in March of 1877 where he became involved in mining. Irish born John W. "Captain Jack" Crawford, the famous "poet scout" of the West, was one of the founders of Custer and a resident of Deadwood. He served as the chief scout for General Crook. Among his most noteworthy poems were a tribute to Custer, published soon after the massacre in 1876, and the poem "Only A Miner", which became a traditional mining song, with a cowboy song variation entitled "Only A Cowboy". [29]

A. Cavanaugh established the Highland mine in 1876. The first prospectors in the Galena camp included E.R. Collins, A. Finnegan, and David Galvin. Among the first settlers of Spearfish in the spring of 1876 were W.W. Bradley, and his brothers, T.K. and F.K., R.H. Evans, and J. Powers.[30] The first merchant in Spearfish was J.C. Ryan. Daniel Toomey established a ranch in the Spearfish valley in May of 1876. In 1877, the first tavern and lunch room were established by Pete Riley, Anton Gerring, Randolph Kelly, and J. Ryan. Among the first people to locate in Sturgis was J. Dudley. [36] The first post office in Sturgis was established during the winter of 1878-79. A Charles Collins was appointed the first postmaster. No mention is made whether this is the same Charles Collins, the promoter and Brule City resident. Irish born John Scollard was the proprietor of the Hotel Scollard in Sturgis.

John W. "Captain Jack" Crawford, the poet scout, and composer of "Only A Miner". Courtesy of David Strain

On February 26, 1876, a party, which included a John Brennan, established a residence in the foot hills of the eastern Black Hills. [31] This was not the same John Brennan that was by now the editor of the Sioux City Times. For many years historians believed that they were one and the same person. Ironically, there were two John Brennans who played an important role in the white settlement of the Hills. Brennan laid out the town site of Rapid City. At the time of the city's incorporation, Brennan was elected president of the City Council. He served nine years as the first postmaster for Rapid City. He eventually became the owner of the American House hotel. [31]

Another early resident of the Rapid Creek area was Mike Quinn, who, as previously mentioned, was a member of O'Neill's second excursion into Canada. Soon after his arrival in the Hills, Quinn established a dray line from Pierre to Rapid to bring supplies to the mining population.[32] He would later establish cattle operations in the Rapid area. The center of this operation was the town of Quinn which was named after Mike. Irish born James Keenan, and Michael McGuire arrived in Rapid City in 1877. They established a saw mill

John Brennan's American House Hotel, Rapid City. Courtesy of the Montana Historical Society.

to provide lumber for the new settlement. Thomas Sweeney located in Rapid City in 1877. By 1879, he had established a hardware business that became one of the largest such enterprises in the Black Hills.

On January 5, 1880, Collins resigned as Brule County Register of Deeds. On January 5, 1881, Charles Collins sold the Brule City site to his wife, Annie. Charley had married Annie Dunn during his stay in the Black Hills. They first met when both were residents of Sioux City. They returned to Sioux City soon after their wedding. Collins travelled to Ireland in 1881 as the Immigration Agent for the Chicago, Milwaukee, and St. Paul Railroad. Upon his return to Sioux City in the autumn of 1881, he revived the Daily Times and once again became its editor. He restored its readership to its previous numbers.

During 1885, Collins fell victim to an assault on a street corner of Sioux City. He suffered permanent injuries as a result and was never able to return to his newspaper work. In 1891, following the suggestions of his doctors that a different climate might improve his physical condition, Charley and Annie moved to San Diego, California.

On February 2, 1892, the Brule City property was sold to John Brennan of Woodbury County, Iowa. Charles Collins purchased

Charles Collins, newspaper editor and land agent. Courtesy of the Sioux City Public Museum.

some property in California and apparently did well in land speculation. He never regained his health. He died in San Diego, California in July of 1893.[32]

1   George Kingsbury, Kingsbury's History of South Dakota, (Yankton, South Dakota), 1915), S. J. Clarke, Chicago, Illinois, Pp. 526-527.

2   The November 21, 1872, Dakota Republican, noted that on December 1, a 100 page book by John Brennan would be published. The title would be Land of the Landless. I have not come across any further reference to this book. There is a question when and where, if at all, it was published.

3   George Kingsbury, Kingsbury's History of South Dakota.

4   Lennox File, Diocese of Sioux Falls Archives.

5   Lennox File, Diocese of Sioux Falls Archives.

6   Perkins Bros., History of Southeastern Dakota, Sioux City, Iowa, 1880.

7   Patricia Donahoe Fokken, Family History Notes, (Sioux Falls).

8   Land Records, Office of the Register of Deeds, Minnehaha County, Sioux Falls, South Dakota.

9   Perkins Bros, History of Southeastern Dakota, Sioux City, Iowa, 1880.

10 Montrose File, Diocese of Sioux Falls Archives.

11 Perkins Bros., History of South Eastern Dakota, Sioux City, Iowa, 1880.

12 Yankton Sacred Heart Church Archives.

13 Robert F.Karolevitz, Yankton, A Pioneer Past, North Plains Press, Aberdeen, South Dakota, 1978.

14 Peter C. Shannon, Father of the Dakota Codes, The Record, Volume 1, No. 6, November, 1895, (Fargo, North Dakota), Pages 10-11.

15 The Sioux Falls Daily Press, July 22, 1923, Page 1.

16 Perkins Bros, History of Southeastern Dakota, Sioux City, Iowa, 1880.

17 Perkins Bros. History of Southeastern Dakota, Sioux City, Iowa, 1880.

18 Hurley, Swan Lake Files, Diocese of Sioux Falls Archives.

19 Military Records of Michael O'Shea, National Archives, Washington, D.C.

20 Carleton Kenyon, History of Ft. Randall, (Department of

History in the Graduate School, U. of South Dakota, Vermillion, 1950), Pp. 71-75, 91-92, 119-120.

21   John Kirwin, Kirwin Family Records.

22   The best, detailed account of the creation and activity at Brule City settlement is found in Dr. Philip Hall's "The Promoter's Trail", Dakota Heritage, Parts I-IV, Ft. Pierre, South Dakota, 1971. Various portions of this account were taken from Philip Hall's series of articles.

23   Philip Hall, "The Promoter's Trail, Dakota Heritage, Ft. Pierre, South Dakota, 1971.

24   Philip Hall, "The Promoter's Trail, Dakota Heritage, Ft. Pierre, South Dakota, 1971.

25   John Brennan, "Dakota's Invitation", Saltiel, P. 58.

26   Annie Tallent, The Black Hills Or the Last Hunting Grounds of the Dakotahs, Centennial Edition, 1876-1976, Brevet Press, Sioux Falls, 1974.

27   Father Peter Rosen, Pa-Sa-Pa or the Black Hills of South Dakota, (St. Louis, 1895), P. 309-475.

28   Father Peter Rosen, Pa-Sa-Pa or the Black Hills of South Dakota (St. Louis, 1895).

29   Archie Green, Only A Miner, University of Illinois Press, Champaign-Urbana, Illinois, 1973.

30   Father Peter Rosen, Pa-Sa-Pa or the Black Hills of South Dakota, (St. Louis, 1895).

31   John Brennan Family History Notes, (Rapid City, South Dakota).

32   Newspaper clipping, Michael Quinn, Rapid City Journal, no date.

33   Charles Collins' obituary appeared in the August 1, 1893, Sioux City Journal.

CHAPTER 4

FURTHER SETTLEMENT
IN THE BLACK HILLS

With the formalization of the opening of the Black Hills in 1877, the mining camps began to organize into more structured communities. At the same time, the economic structure of the mining industry became more centralized. Large mining operations, such as the Homestake Mine in Lead, became the order of the day. Communities and livestock operations among the foothills of the Black Hills became more organized as well. Many Irish American men, perhaps because the cowboy lifestyle was similar to their role as an Irish peasant, were involved in the initial cattle operations established to provide meat for the expanding mining population. These events would influence the pattern of Irish settlement in West River for the period 1877 to 1889. The majority of the land west of the Missouri River remained part of the Great Sioux Reservation until 1889, however.

There was extensive Irish involvement in the establishment of mining communities in the Black Hills. The mining camp along Silver Creek was first established by John and Tom Gorman in 1876. The site was first called Gorman Camp and eventually changed to Silver City. [32] John discovered the Diana Lode. With his brother, Tom, he began placer mining and construction of a permanent mining settlement. By 1878 the estimated population of Silver City region, which extended along Rapid Creek, was 300. Patrick Gorman joined the Gorman brothers in 1881. The Gormans, as well as Mark Duggan, who had arrived in the area in 1876, were all Irish American. The Catholic Church in Silver City, its wooden structure still in use, was constructed by the Irish population.[1]

The Irish were found in several communities throughout the Hills. Due in part to discrimination in hiring, the Irish were given the most dangerous and difficult jobs in the mining operations. As previously noted, the Irish were among those who possessed

technical knowledge of hardrock mining operations. The Irish
population was significant enough to aid in the creation of Catholic
Church congregations at Lead, Central City, and Deadwood.
[29,28,27] Lead's church was named for St. Patrick. The Central
City church was named in honor of St. Lawrence O'Toole, an Irish
Bishop from the late middle ages.

Crook City, like many communities in the eastern portion of
Dakota, was a victim of the coming of the railroad. [33] The railroad

*The Central City mining camp included St. Lawrence O'Toole's
Catholic Church and the residences of many Irish American
families. Courtesy of the South Dakota Historical Society.*

was built in the Northern Hills in 1879. Because the railroad engineers were unable to locate a grade that would follow from Crook City into the Hills toward Deadwood, the train line was located four miles from the settlement site. Within days the settlement of Whitewood developed. Many of the settlers were Irish American. The Catholic community was predominantly Irish. A permanent church was never established. However, a congregation, which maintained a house for use as a church, functioned throughout this period. Among the Irish congregation members were: Gallagher, a hardware store owner, Thomas O'Connor, J. O'Callaghan, M. Fowler, Elijah Fowler, Patrick Cusick, Patrick Conlin, Thomas McNally, Judge Brennan, James Hunt, J.L. Deman, A. McLain, John Burke, J. Mulvaney, J.O. Chasse, John Breslin, and James Muldoon. The major fund raiser for the congregation was an annual St. Patrick's Day dance. [2]

The Irish contingent of Custer grew with the arrival of E.P. Walsh and wife in 1883. [30] Also arriving were: John and Mike Mallon and their wives, and the Jeremiah Horigan family. The Deadwood Catholic congregation, named for St. Ambrose, included members: John Treber, Peter O'Neill, M. Murphy, Henry McGill, Judge Daniel McLaughlin, J.D. Cornell, Neil McDonough, P.D. O'Brien, Thomas Powers, John H. Russell, John Holiday, Sheriff John Manning, Edward McDonald, T.L. Skinner, Mrs. Catherine Allen, James Curran, Mrs. Molihan, Peter McHugh, John McAlier, Joe Hayes, James Carney, D. Shannon, Henry and James Frawley, residents of the Centennial Valley, and Peter Burns.[3] Judge Daniel McLauglin had been a member of the Nebraska State Legislature, a probate judge in Idaho, and a newspaper editor in Salt Lake City, Utah. He arrived in Deadwood in 1877. His name appears as a director of the St. Ambrose Church in Deadwood from its inception. The Galena community included: Davey Kobie, Katie Doyle and Bart Harris. [34] A Catholic Church was built in 1883.[4] By 1887, the Oelrichs community, the base of a large cattle operation, included families of Dooleys, Crowleys, Humphreys, Mardes and the Arthur Colligan family. Catholic services were held at the Colligan home. [113] Fred T. Evans, who was involved in the freighting business into the Hills, located in Hot Springs. Evans contributed heavily to the establishment of the Catholic Church in Hot Springs.[5] [112] At the time of statehood in 1889, Evans was developing plans for a hospital and possible college to be located near the hot springs. They were to be staffed by Catholic sisters. He also was exploring the tourist and health potential of the hot springs site.

St. Patrick Street, one of the main thoroughfares of Rapid City, is a present day reminder of the presence of Irish men such as John Brennan, Michael Quinn, and George McNamara in the early days of the community. [31] William Mahoney was the St. Mary's Church's resident pastor at the time of statehood in 1889. By 1886, the Catholics of Spearfish were raising funds to build a church. [35] Services were held at the Ford House. The committee was chaired by Grandpa Reilly and Mike Kerwin.

Ft. Meade was established in 1878 as a military outpost to protect settlers into the northern Hills. [36] Like many of the military posts in the region, many of the soldiers were Irish Americans. The Colonel Samuel Sturgis family became Catholics after the death of their son, Jack at the Custer Massacre. Colonel Sturgis assisted Father Peter Rosen, in the construction of a Catholic Church for the residents of Ft. Meade. The town which formed around the fort was named in honor of the Colonel. Another contribution to the Catholic community in Sturgis was the proprietor of the local house of ill fame, "Poker" Alice Tubbs.[6] Poker Alice had been raised in a Catholic convent in England. She remained Catholic throughout her life. She attempted to contribute money to the church at various times but was turned down by the local pastor. She did spend considerable time praying and giving special offerings at the church. She was perhaps an Irish Catholic born in England. Another of the legendary characters of the early Black Hills who was Irish was "Lame Johnny" Donohoe. Donohoe came to the Hills as a prospector in the last years of the gold rush.

The Irish Religious, both Catholic sisters and priests, played an important role in the early settlements in the Black Hills. During the spring of 1877, Joseph Treanor petitioned Bishop James O'Connor of Omaha for a priest to live in Deadwood. In May of 1877, Bishop

O'Connor sent John Lonergan, an Irish born, Holy Cross priest, to Deadwood. Father Lonergan supervised the construction of a Catholic Church. He was replaced in the fall of 1877 by P.N. O'Brien who remained a short time. Father Bernard Mackin, an Irish born diocesan priest from Nebraska, was then sent to Deadwood in February of 1878. During the summer of 1878, Sisters of the Holy Cross, from St. Mary's, Indiana were sent to Deadwood. Selected were Sisters Edward Murphy, Matilda Hartnett, Marciana O'Sullivan, Basilla Thornton, and Passion Crowley. Soon after their arrival, a benefit program for the hospital fund was presented at the Langrishe Theatre. By the end of the summe,r the Sisters had started hospitals in both Lead and Deadwood. A permanent brick structure was started in Deadwood in the summer of 1879.[7] Soon after the Sisters' arrival, Father Mackin invited Holy Cross Fathers from Notre Dame, Indiana to serve in the Black Hills.

During the summer of 1879, Irish born Father John Toohey was sent to assist Bernard Mackin. Martin Marty was made Catholic Bishop of the Vicariate of Dakota in the fall of 1879. Catholic Church jurisdiction was placed under the Vicariate of Dakota.

The Irish presence in the early days of Deadwood was extensive. Courtesy of the South Dakota Historical Society.

Several Holy Cross Fathers worked as missionaries under Bishop Marty. Father Toohey helped to begin a St. Patrick's Day celebration in Deadwood in March of 1878. Father Mackin died during the winter of 1879-80, after contracting a virus while riding between missions in the Black Hills.[8] Katherine Mackin Callahan, Father Mackin's widow sister, with her son, Patrick had been living with Father Mackin. The Callahans were forced to move out into the Black Hills and live off of game they could kill. Katherine eventually located work as the washerwoman for the soldiers at Fort Meade.

Irish born Father James Gleeson was sent from Notre Dame to replace Mackin. Irish born John Shea, and Richard Maher were to follow Father Gleeson. Father Maher began St. Edward's Academy in Deadwood in 1883. Seventeen different Irish sisters taught at St. Edward's in the period 1883 to 1897.

Bishop Marty visited the Black Hills in 1880. The population had grown to over 13,000 people. Deadwood had a population of an estimated 3,677 people. Father Patrick Colovin arrived in Deadwood during this time, as did, but only for a short period, the Presentation Sisters, led by Mother Hughes.

*James Gleeson, (left page)
and Patrick Colovin,
(right page) the Holy Cross
Fathers from Notre Dame,
Indiana served the Irish
residents of the Black Hills
during the territorial period.
Courtesy of the Indiana
Province Archives Center,
Notre Dame, Indiana.*

The next Holy Cross missionary to be sent to the Black Hills was Peter Rosen in September, 1882. Unlike his predecessors Rosen was German and not Irish. This, however, did not affect Rosen's activities in developing parishes in the northern Hills. Rosen withdrew from the Holy Cross Fathers and became a diocesan priest when the Holy Cross Order withdrew from the Dakota Territory in 1886. Rosen remained in the diocese until the early 1890's.

After Rosen left the Black Hills, he published a history of the early settlement of the Hills, <u>Pa-Ha-Sap-Pa or the The Black Hills of Dakota.</u> The text is still considered one of the best detailed accounts of early activity in the region. Rosen participated in a Catholic Church dispute that involved the Irish Catholic miners of the Hills. Several of the parishioners in the Hills belonged to the miner's union. The Third Baltimore Council of 1884 changed the Church's law, making it a sin to belong to a secret society. Father Rosen believed that membership in a miners union, with its necessarily secret meetings and membership rolls violated the ban against secret societies. Father Rosen sent inquiries and a copy of one of the

miners' union constitution to his superior, Bishop Martin Marty. After reading the union constitution, Marty stated "that having secrets alone was not a cause for condemnation and no theological problems were posed by the constitution. As long as union members consult their priests on matters of conscience there could be no objection to organizing for self protection." They were also instructed to eliminate any religious rituals from their ceremonies. Peter Rosen would eventually moved to Minnesota. This issue apparently was reviewed by John Ireland, who by this time had become Archbishop of St. Paul, with jurisdiction over Dakota. Archbishop Ireland's position remained similar to Bishop Marty. The secret society question became a major issue within the Catholic Church in the 1890s. Rosen would publish a text, The Catholic Church and Secret Societies, which hoped to expose the sinfulness of such societies and the apparent approval of their membership by Archbishop Ireland.[9] The condemnation of secret societies in the *Dakota Catholic* in 1889 was in response to this question.

There is evidence that the Irish Nationalist organization, the Clan an Gael, had a chapter in Lead.[10] The Clan an Gael supported the efforts of the Land League in bringing about land reform in Ireland. Funds from the organization were also used to carry out bombings against British officials and institutions. The Clan an Gael also had a chapter in Sioux City, Iowa.

1   A Century of History of Silver City, 1876 - 1976 (Silver City, South Dakota, 1976), Page 1-2, 9.

2   Ledger, Whitewood Congregation, Whitewood File, Diocese of Rapid City Archives, Rapid City, South Dakota.

3   Historical Notes, Deadwood, St. Ambrose File, Diocese of Rapid City Archives, Rapid City, South Dakota.

4   J. S. McClintock, Pioneer Days in the Black Hills (Deadwood, South Dakota, 1939), Biographical sketches.

5   J. S. McClintock, Pioneer Days in the Black Hills (Deadwood, South Dakota, 1937.

6   Sturgis File, Diocese of Rapid City Archives.

7   Brother Franklin Cullen, C.S.C., Holy Cross In The Black Hills, The Dakota Apostolates, 1878-1897, (Brothers of the Holy Cross, Mountain View, California, 1986), Pages 4-29.

8   Interview with Tom Callahan, Rapid City, 1989.

9   Sister M. Claudia Duratschek, O.S.B., The Beginnings of Catholicism in South Dakota, (The Catholic University Press, Washington, D.C., 1943), Pages 198-209.

10   Joseph Cash, Mining the Homestake, (University of Iowa Press, Iowa City, 1975), Page 69.

CHAPTER 5

FORMAL COLONIZATION EFFORTS

The Irish Emigration Society was first organized in St. Paul, Minnesota on May 12, 1864. Father John Ireland was its first president. Dillon O'Brien was its first secretary. For the next decade, speeches by Ireland, O'Brien, and guests, such as Thomas Meagher, were given periodically throughout the region in support of Irish colonization in the West. In 1875, John Ireland was appointed adjunct bishop of the Catholic Diocese of St. Paul. In his new position Bishop Ireland was permitted to develop his ideas on colonization in a more formal manner.[1]

In 1875, Bishop Ireland proposed to the representatives of the bankrupt Northern Pacific Railroad that he become a land agent for the First Division St. Paul and Pacific Railroad. With no expense to the railroad, other than land agent's commission, Bishop Ireland used his position to publicize the establishment of land colonies specifically organized for Catholic settlement.

On January 22, 1876, Ireland created the Catholic Colonization Bureau to replace the Irish Emigration Society. It was to be administered by Dillon O'Brien. Ireland was given, by the St. Paul and Pacific Railroad, land agent powers over 23,040 acres in Swift County, Minnesota. By 1879, the colony would be comprised of 117,000 acres. The towns of Clontarf and DeGraff were created along the established rail line.

In 1877, the Catholic Colonization Bureau Colony at Adrian, Minnesota was established. Father Christian Knauf was appointed as the resident pastor and land agent. The Black Hills branch of the St. Paul and Sioux City Railroad built a railroad through Murray County, just north of Nobles County and the Adrian settlement. Bishop Ireland was assigned 52,000 acres of land in Murray County. The Avoca Colony was established on this site. Besides the Avoca settlement, Iona, Fulda, Currie, and Graceville settlements were established.[2]

In May and July, 1879, Bishop Ireland established contracts with the Winona and St. Paul Railroad Company to create colonies in Lyons County, Minnesota. Colonies at Minneota and outside of Marshall, Minnesota were established. In 1878, James J. Hill, his wife an Irish Catholic immigrant, was appointed general manager of the reorganized St. Paul, Minneapolis, and Manitoba Railroad. On December 31, 1879, Hill put Bishop Ireland in charge of 50,000 acres of land in Big Stone and Traverse Counties, Minnesota. In June, 1879, a wealthy Irish landowner, John Sweetman, through contacts with Bishop Ireland, purchased 10,000 acres of land in Murray County, Minnesota. By June, 1880, land contracts for Catholic Colonization Bureau settlements involving over 379,000 acres of land had been established.

In 1876, the jurisdiction of the Diocese of St. Paul included all of Dakota Territory east of the Missouri. During the summer of 1876, Bishop Ireland traveled to Yankton, Dakota Territory, to visit the mission parishes, administer the sacraments, assist in special temperance missions, and survey the region for possible Catholic settlement. Although the Bureau's _1879 Emigrant Guide Book_ included South Minnesota and Eastern Dakota in its descriptions, no formal Catholic Colonization Bureau settlements were established in

Father John Ireland, first president of the Irish Immigration Society. Courtesy of the Archives of the Archdiocese of St. Paul and Minneapolis.

Dakota Territory.[3] The <u>Catholic Directory of 1879</u> does note, however, that a priest from the Adrian colony, Father Christian Knauf, served missions at Sioux Falls and Lennox. Priests from the Avoca settlement visited the Flandreau and Brookings missions.

The quirks of geography and the change of the name of the colonization organization in 1876 have led to great confusion among historians on the pattern of settlement developed under the formal organization. Sister Claudia Duratschek suggested that strays from these organized, Catholic colonies wandered across the border into Dakota Territory as single family units. She believed that in most cases the Catholic families lost their religion, due to the lack of a resident pastor.[4] Considering the number of Irish Catholic families in Sioux Falls which can trace their arrival in the region to participation in these organized efforts, this writer cannot agree with Sister Claudia's assertions.

In following the descriptions of the establishment of these colonies one must realize the close association of the Irish to the Catholic faith. Also, more importantly, is the fact that Bishop Ireland changed the name of the colonization organization from the Irish Emmigration Society to the Catholic Colonization Bureau. This was done to include the various ethnic groups; Germans, Swiss, Belgians, and French, which were involved with the Irish in the Catholic Colonization effort in the West. Bishop John Spalding would note in his book, that the Irish colonies, beginning with the few German Catholic settlers involved in the 1855, St. John City effort, were not exclusively, Irish in composition. For that matter approximately ten per cent of the Irish settlers in Dakota were not Catholic.

These rural colonies, centered around the church's activities, were attempts at preserving the true spirituality of Irish Catholicism and rescuing Catholic immigrants, especially the Irish immigrants from the slums of the eastern cities.

Perhaps the most publicized of these colonization efforts was John Sweetman's activities in the development of the Sweetman Catholic Colony of Currie, Minnesota. John Sweetman, a wealthy, Catholic landowner and philanthropist living in Ireland, was involved in the founding of the Land League in October, 1879. He personally nominated Charles Parnell for the presidency.[5] In 1879 and 1880. famine returned to portions of Ireland. Fear of starvation like that of the Great Famine developed. Sweetman began special work projects on his lands in County Meath. He also became interested in an organized effort at colonization in America. Sweetman travelled to America in the spring of 1880. He came in contact with Dillon O'Brien while visiting St. Paul. O'Brien, Bishop Ireland, and Sweetman developed the idea of removing Irish residents from the famine areas of Ireland and locating them in a Catholic Colonization Bureau colony. In a search for the ideal location for the colony, Sweetman traveled to the Red River Valley on the Minnesota-Dakota border. He surveyed land in Bismarck, and along the James River, near Jamestown, in the northern portion of Dakota Territory. He proceeded then to Watertown, Dakota. The area near Goodwin, Dakota, that he checked out was suffering through a severe drought. As a result, he chose the site of Currie on the Minnesota-Dakota border.

Irish peasants, some still emaciated from near starvation in County Conamara, Ireland, were transported directly from Ireland to the new colony. The physically weakened immigrants, most with little or no farming experience, were expected to become instant homesteaders on the open prairie. The severe winter of 1880-81 drove many of the new colony's immigrants quickly away from the colony. The failure of the Sweetman colony, especially, because of the wide publicity that it had received, greatly upset Dillon O'Brien and Bishop John Ireland.

Bishop James O'Connor and John O'Neill continued their colonization efforts in Nebraska. During the winter of 1873 and into the spring of 1874, General John O'Neill spoke throughout the country encouraging Irish Americans to move to a proposed colony in Nebraska Territory.[6] At this time the planned, O'Neill City was little more than a few scattered structures. As part of the promotional effort, O'Neill circulated flyers describing, in detail, the routes to the planned colony. The first settlers in the Holt County settlement arrived on May 12, 1874. [26] The group consisted of 23

men, women, and children. O'Neill brought two other groups into
O'Neill City in 1874 and 1875. An additional 71 men arrived in
April, 1877. O'Neill's previously quoted speech of December 6,
1876, gave an explanation of the ultimate intent of O'Neill for the
formation of the colony.

During the first months of 1876, James O'Gorman, the Catholic
Bishop of Omaha, Nebraska died. He was replaced by James
O'Connor, a priest from the Philadelphia, Pennsylvania area. Like
O'Gorman, O'Connor was an Irish American. Contained in Bishop
O'Connor's letters in the Archdiocese of Omaha's Archives are
letters from John O'Neill to the new bishop. The first letter, dated
December 27, 1876, and addressed from the Head Quarters
O'Neill's Irish American Colonies, Philadelphia, Pa., explains the
status of O'Neill's colonization efforts.

O'Neill expressed the belief that he was engaged in one of the
best works that could be undertaken by a lay Catholic. He described
his activities as "encouraging, directing and assisting the Irish
people in leave the overcrowded cities and States of the East and
settling upon the cheap and free lands of the West, where, by
economy and industry, in a few years become happy and
comfortable".

O'Neill summarized his activities in the past five years. He
believed that there were millions of Irish people in "the mines,
workshops, and the cellars and garrets of the larger cities, who could
better their condition by settling upon and cultivating the land". He
stated that the first two years of his colonization efforts brought little
success. He had perceived economic and political changes during
1876 that led to an enormous interest in the colonization of the West.
O'Neill went on to present a step-by-step colonization process on
either, government or railroad lands. He hoped to create a dozen
colonies during 1877 on the plains of Nebraska. O'Neill hoped to
have a resident priest at each colony to attend to religious duties.

Although his residence was in Nebraska, O'Neill spent much of
his time in the East promoting the colonization effort. His letter of
February 14, 1877, with a Wilkes-Barre, Pennsylvania address,
began with reassurances that O'Neill would "at all times endeavor to

be worthy of Bishop O'Connor's kindness." He also referred to a "patriotic provision" mentioned in Bishop O'Connor's previous letter that would placate O'Connor's fear that O'Neill would "undertake anything in the direction which sound judgment and prudent counsel would not sanction". Was O'Neill swearing off armed attacks against English possessions? This sentiment was in sharp contrast with comments in his speech presented the previous December, that encouraged further attacks on England from a string of colonies along the northern boundaries of America. Perhaps, O'Neill did give up his desire to once again attack Canada.

O'Neill would not live to see but the beginnings of his plans. O'Neill, who suffered from asthma, developed pneumonia in November, 1877. He suffered a stroke and later died on January 8, 1878, of further complications of the illness. O'Neill was only 44 years of age at the time of his death.

Ironically, William B. O'Donaghue, by this time an established school teacher in Farmington, Minnesota, would die in March, 1877 of tuberculosis at the age of 35.[7] It is difficult to speculate what would have transpired if O'Donaghue and O'Neill had both not died at such an early age.

Omaha Bishop James O'Gorman (left page) and his successor, James O'Connor (right page) encouraged Irish settlement in the region. Courtesy of the Archives of the Archdiocese of Omaha.

Bishop James O'Connor would continue O'Neill's plans for colonization in Nebraska. In 1879 Bishop O'Connor assisted in the organization of the Irish Colonization Association. Plans for organized colonies like those in Minnesota were developed. The colony of O'Connor and the town of Erina, under the direction of the Boston Colonization Society were established in 1880. These settlements developed along with the Greeley Center, Spalding and O'Neill settlements in Greeley County.[8]

The western portion of what became Dakota Territory was under the Catholic Church jurisdiction of the Vicariate of Nebraska. Martin Marty, along with Meinrad McCarthy served as the missionary to the Plains Indians for the Vicariate. Their superior was the Bishop of Omaha. In the fall of of 1879, Marty was made bishop of the newly created Vicariate of Dakota. Soon after the appointment, Meinrad McCarthy, from the Sacred Heart's settlement near Bon Homme, Dakota Territory, wrote his former superior, Bishop O'Connor. In the letter, he discussed the building of churches in the Bon Homme area and the possible location of a

monastery and convent within the Catholic settlements along the east bank of the Missouri River in Dakota. [14]

Like McCarthy, Marty continued to correspond with Bishop O'Connor. In a letter dated February 25, 1880, Marty believed that it would be advisable to build a school along the "East-side of the Missouri River among the Canadians whose children are half-breeds." Marty, along with fellow missionary, Father J.F. Malo wanted the "Nuns from Ireland" to operate the school, as a "means to gain a lasting & effedical sympathy among the most numerous & generous class of our people." The Nuns were the Presentation Sisters from Ireland.

In a letter dated, June 30, 1880, Marty commented to Bishop O'Connor that the Presentation Sisters had been located at St. Ann's Mission, near the Wheeler settlement. [43] He believed that "The Country on the Eastside of the Missouri in that same neighborhood would also be admissible for a Catholic Colony." Marty commented that, "Before we say anything about it," ...they must "see how you come out of your so well directed enterprise in Greeley Co.".

In 1880 Bishop Martin Marty was appointed by the directors of the Catholic Colonization Association to a committee for the

Martin Marty, missionary to Dakota, and later the first bishop of the Vicariate of Dakota. Courtesy of the Archives of the Diocese of Sioux Falls.

"location of desirable tracts of land" for settlement. Later, in 1884, during the Third Council of Baltimore, Marty spoke at a Colonization Association meeting attended by Bishops Ireland and Spalding. Bishop Marty discussed the advantages Dakota provided to prospective immigrants. No formal settlement was ever created in Dakota Territory.[9]

The Presentation Sisters would play an important role in Irish settlement in Dakota. Bishop James O'Gorman had spent time with the Presentation Sisters of the Blessed Virgin while a young cleric in Ireland. Correspondence in the Omaha Archdiocese Archives between Sister DeSales Carrick, mother superior of the Presentation Sisters, and Bishop is dated as early as December 30, 1877. In that letter Sister DeSales mentioned that she was writing concerning the "projected mission among your poor Indians". A clergyman had fully discussed the matter with their Cardinal and the Cardinal had "blessed and entirely approved the project". Certain sisters were prepared to carry out the mission. For nearly two years, correspondence to Bishop O'Connor included inquiries about when exactly they were to be coming to the mission. Finally, Martin Marty, in the fall of 1879, on his return home from Rome after his consecration as Bishop of the Vicariate of Dakota, stopped in Dublin, Ireland. He escorted the volunteers, Sister M. John Hughes, her blood sister, M. Agnes Hughes, and Sister Teresa McCarthy, to a mission convent that had been established near Wheeler in Charles Mix County, Dakota. The convent was actually an earthen hut. The Sisters spent the winter teaching the children of the community. In the spring of 1880, the walls of the earthen structure began to collapse. Sister Teresa McCarthy returned to Ireland. After viewing the situation Bishop Marty decided to send the remaining sisters to Deadwood to start a school for the children of the miners. After it was determined that Sunday Mass could not be said in their convent, and not being impressed with the conditions of the mining town, the sisters returned to Yankton. They were housed temporarily with the Sisters of Mercy in Yankton.

After fifteen months in Yankton, the Sisters moved to Fargo, Dakota Territory, where they established a residence. Additional

volunteers from Ireland had arrived. In 1886, at the urging of Father
Robert Haire, the Presentation Sisters founded a convent in
Aberdeen, Dakota Territory. At this time, the Presentation Sisters
began to educate the children of the Catholic immigrants. They did
not return until the 1980s to educating Native Americans. The
author is a product of the Presentation Sisters' tradition of
education.

Another group of Irish Sisters, the Sisters of Mercy, were
participants in the Irish settlement in Dakota. Bishop James
O'Connor sent five sisters, M. Gabriel Mahoney, M. Frances
Campbell, M. Genevieve Sheridan, M. DeSales Garaghty, M. Paul
Ewins, M. Angela McCarthy and M. Ignatius Lynch, from the
Sisters of Mercy Convent in Omaha to Yankton in August of 1878.

The Sisters opened Sacred Heart Academy and within a year
completed construction of a building which opened in June of 1880.
The Academy was in financial problems from the beginning.
Further problems arose when one of the Sisters, Sister Mary Paul
Kerns, married Dr. V. Sebiakin-Ross, a local physician. The scandal
caused the already insufficient funding for the school to disappear
rapidly.[10] The academy soon closed. The Sisters of Mercy returned

*Mother M. John Hughes led
the establishment of the
Presentation Sisters in
Dakota Territory. Courtesy
of the Archives of the
Presentation Sisters.*

to Omaha. Mary Paul and Dr. Ross remained for many years in Yankton. Dr. Ross would later be involved with the organization of Sacred Heart Hospital in Yankton. They later moved to Sioux Falls.[11]

As was stated in the introduction, Peoria's Bishop John Spalding believed the settlement of the Irish in the west was a religious mission. Spalding was selected as Catholic Bishop of the newly created Diocese of Peoria, Illinois in 1875. He soon became an active participant in the affairs of midwestern Catholics. His activities in encouraging Irish settlement in the West led to the endorsement of the concept of the spiritual revival of the Irish Catholics through the establishment of rural communities in the West.[12]

Dillon O'Brien of St. Paul and William Onahan of Chicago, both participants in a colonization convention in St.Louis in 1869, convinced Bishop John Ireland of St. Paul to call for another national convention to be held in conjunction with the annual gathering of the St. Patrick's Society in Chicago in March of 1879.

The St. Patrick's Society was a fraternal organization that included many veteran, Irish American politicians like its president, William Onahan. It was not as Annie Tallent suggested, a clandestine, revolutionary organization. Unlike the 1869 convention these meetings developed into an active colonization organization. John Spalding did not attend the Chicago convention, but was later invited by Bishop John Ireland to the organizational meetings of the Irish Catholic Colonization Association of the United States. The meeting included five Catholic Bishops. They were: Ireland, O'Connor, Spalding, Louis Fink of Leavenworth, Kansas, and John Hogan of Kansas City. As a result of the meetings, the Association was incorporated in the state of Illinois as a stock company. Bishop Spalding was elected as the President of the board. Officers included Anthony Kelley, vice-president, William Onahan, secretary and W. J. Quan, treasurer. The executive committee consisted of John Lawler, P.J. Towle, Fathers, P.J. Conway and D.J. Riordan and Bishops O'Connor and Ireland. The Board of Directors included Archbishop James Gibbons of Baltimore, Bishop John J. Williams,

Father Stephen Byrne, John Boyle O'Reilly, P.H. Hickey, Henry Hoguet, Dan Foley and John Fitzgerald of Lincoln, Nebraska. Spalding remained the president until the Association was dissolved.

Spalding presented speeches throughout the country, encouraging Catholic colonization in the west. In these speeches, Spalding presented the concept of the Irish having a special mission of reviving Catholicism in the English-speaking world. They could only carry this out by returning to the land and forming communities in which farming was the main occupation, and the local Catholic Church, the center of the social and religious life of the residents.

The Colonization Association, through the direction of Bishop O'Connor of Omaha, took control of the continuing development of the Greeley Colony in Nebraska. They assisted in the financing of colonies in Arkansas and Minnesota. The Association would continue in operation into the mid 1880s.

The Association's efforts would put the seal of the Irish Catholic, religious and political leaders on the concept of Irish settlement in the West. The Irish of Dakota played a key role in these events.

1   "Archbishop Ireland's Colonies", <u>Acta Et Dicta</u> (Archdiocese of St. Paul, St. Paul, Minnesota, 1934), Pages 212-231.

2   "Archbishop Ireland's Colonies", <u>Acta Et Dicta</u>, (Archdiocese of St. Paul, St. Paul, Minnesota, 1934), Pages 212-231.

3   Sister M. Claudia Duratschek, O. S. B., <u>Builders of God's Kingdom</u>, (Yankton, South Dakota 1979), Page 33.

4   Sister M. Claudia Duratschek, O. S. B., <u>Builders of God's Kingdom,</u> (Yankton, South Dakota, 1879), Page 33.

5   John Sweetman, "The Sweetman Colony of Currie, Minnesota: A Memoir", <u>Acta Et Dicta, Volume 3</u>, (Archdiocese of St. Paul, St. Paul, 1911), Pages 41-65.

6   Gregory Y. Passewitz, <u>History of Greeley County, O'Neill, Nebraska</u>.

7   Family notes, John O'Connell Family, (Minnesota State Historical Society, St. Paul), Pages 197-199.

8   Gregory R. Passewitz, "O'Neill, Nebraska, The First Quarter Century", <u>History of Greeley County, O'Neill, Nebraska</u>, Pages 5-8.

9   Sister M. Claudia Duratschek, O.S.B., <u>The Beginnings of Catholicism in South Dakota</u>, (Catholic University of America, Washington, D. D., 1943), Pages 245-246.

10   Henry Casper, S.J., <u>The History of the Catholic Church in Nebraska</u>, (Bruce Press, Milwaukee, 1960), Pages 230-262.

11   Robert Karolevitz, <u>Yankton, A Pioneer Past</u>, (North Plains Press, Aberdeen, South Dakota, 1972), Page 111.

12   David Francis Sweeney, <u>The Life of John Lancaster Spalding</u>, (New York, 1965), Pages 109-155.

CHAPTER 6

MCCALL AND THE MYTH
OF THE WILD IRISHMEN

This study has examined several instances in which an Irish American was accused of a major crime. During this period, there was a belief that the Irish were inherently lawless and uncivilized. The William Barry incident, and the failure to prosecute the Fenian raid at Pembina seemed to have nurtured this myth. The arrival of Peter Shannon, a law and order, Irish-American judge, was quite important. The successful prosecution of the murderer of Will Bill Hickok, Jack McCall, was another incident in the continued attempt at bringing the wild Irishmen of the frontier to justice.

The murder and hanging of Jack McCall were quite famous incidents in South Dakota and the history of the West. Jack McCall killed Bill Hickok in Deadwood in 1876. He was first tried in a provisional court in Deadwood. The jury was made up of fellow gold miners. How many were Irish? A list of jurors is not available. He was acquitted. After he continued to brag about his exploit, he was once again arrested and taken to Yankton for trial, much like Barry in the previous decade. He was convicted in Peter Shannon's courtroom and sentenced to hang.

Several of the Protestant clergy offered to assist McCall in preparing his soul for the other world. McCall demanded that he be able to see a Catholic priest. This was at the time when Father Lechlietner had left the region. A Catholic priest from near by St. Helena, Nebraska was brought to McCall's cell. Father Sommereisen prepared McCall for his death. McCall was hung in March of 1877. He was buried in the Sacred Heart Catholic Cemetery.[1]

Interestingly, Bailey's History of Minnehaha County, published in 1899, describes five famous trials in the county's short history. Three of the five involve Irish residents. The murder of the Seventh Cavalry officer, Casey, an Irish American, by Plenty Horses after the Wounded Knee Massacre, is one of the other cases.[2]

The most publicized case was the alleged murder of Mary Egan by her husband, Thomas Egan, in September, 1880. Thomas Egan, a native of County Tipperary, Ireland, was charged with strangling his wife at their recently established homestead in the northwest portion of Minnehaha County. Egan was taken to trial in Sioux Falls, where he was convicted and sentenced to be hanged. After several appeals, Thomas Egan was hung in Sioux Falls on July 13, 1882. The date was moved up from an original Friday date at the request of Thomas Egan's priest, William Maher. The execution received special mention in newspapers throughout the country, including the *New York Times,* of July 14, 1882.[3] The reason that it received the attention was the gruesome method in which he was executed. Thomas Egan was a rather large man. It took three different attempts at springing the trap door and two broken ropes before Egan was finally killed. The *Times'* account noted that this was the first and perhaps the last execution of its kind in Dakota Territory. There were, however, many other subsequent hangings. Even more tragic was the death bed confession on June 3, 1927, of Thomas Egan's stepdaughter, Catherine Van Horn, to the murder of her mother, Mary Egan. Thomas Egan had confessed his innocence until his execution.[4]

1   Robert Karolevitz, <u>Yankton, A Pioneer Past </u>(North Plains Press, Aberdeen, South Dakota, 1972), Pages 84-85.

2   Dana Bailey, <u>History of Minnehaha County</u> (Sioux Falls, 1899), Pages 230-31.

3   *New York Times*, July 14, 1882.

4   John Egan, <u>Catherine's Confession</u> (Sioux Falls, 1988), Page 16.

CHAPTER 7

THE COMING OF THE RAILROAD AND THE DAKOTA BOOM: THE EFFECTS ON IRISH SETTLEMENT

The initial settlements in eastern Dakota that included Irish people were developed along rivers and streams and along the military roads from Sioux City to the Missouri River and from the Minnesota border to Yankton. The building of railroads into the region determined the continued existence of the settlements. It also brought an influx of many more Irish immigrants. Either as workers, building the railroad, or as homesteaders following the paths established by promoters, such as the Catholic Colonization Bureau in Minnesota and Nebraska.

The Irish settlements at the time of the coming of the railroad included Garryowen and Emmet, in Union County along the Brule Creek. The communities of Wakonda, Stars Corner, and Lodi formed in Clay County in the vicinity of the Bloomingdale settlement, roughly twenty miles up the James River from Vermillion. [40,41,42] The Catholic population was significant enough to have resident pastors at Wakonda, Emmet, and Lodi. The railroads entered Union County at Sioux City. The railroads passed through Elk Point, Jefferson, Wakonda, and Vermillion. Eventually, the communities of Lodi, Star Corners, and Bloomingdale, would cease to exist. The rail lines passed through Beresford and Alcester. Emmet and Garryowen, remained totally farm communities with a Catholic Church and, occasionally, an attempt at a store, the only visible signs of an active community of family homesteads. This type of community was very similar to traditional rural communities in Ireland.

In Turner County, Hurley was connected to the rail line. Swan Lake, however, no longer functioned as a community after the trains bypassed the location. Swan Lake began as an important watering stop on the Yankton to Sioux Falls road. Downer T. Bramble moved to Swan Lake. He served as a Dakota Territorial legislator from Turner County. Most of the townspeople moved into Viborg, along the rail line, nearly eight miles to the southeast.

In Yankton County, the settlement of Walshtown developed to the north of John Stanage's post. Stanage's post was approximately one mile south of present day Mission Hill, along the bluffs east of the James River. St. Bridget's Church in Walshtown had a resident pastor.[1] [39]

Among the parishioners were: Francis Walsh, John Kelly, Michael Gavin and Neil Malloy. St. Kyran's Church in the Mayfield community, ten miles to the north, also included many Irish settlers. St. Kyran's and St. Bridget's were eventually combined into St. Columba's Church of Mayfield. It remains a totally rural congregation.

George Sheehan, Irish born, was the first Catholic priest ordained for Dakota in 1880 in Milwaukee. He was first stationed at Yankton, which at that time was the location of Bishop Martin Marty. Sheehan, who was a Gaelic, English, and French speaker, was the brother of William, the Catholic Bishop of Waterford, Ireland.[2] George organized the parishes at Walshtown, Mayfield, Lodi, Wakonda, Beresford, Clear Lake, White and Davis. He also served in Mitchell, Sioux Falls and Elkton, where he died in retirement. In 1882, Father Sheehan, the pastor of Emmet, Father

The Dakota Southern Railroad brought many Irish settlers to Dakota Territory. Courtesy of Leonard Tripp.

J.J. Shea, along with John Duggan, the superintendent of the Home of Destitute Children in Boston, began the process of bringing orphan Irish children from the streets of Boston into foster homes among the Irish Catholic farmers of eastern Dakota. These efforts received national attention in the Irish American press. Father Sheehan and John Duggan carried out trips through the fall of 1884 transporting at least 96 children to homes in Dakota.

Father Sheehan was quoted in the *Yankton Daily Press and Dakotaian* of September 8, 1883, that the "object in sending these little orphans out in the west territory and states, is to provide them homes and rescue them from vice and sin, which is usually the lot of destitute children in large cities." Father Sheehan also spoke at gatherings sponsored by the Catholic Colonization Society in which he encouraged settlement in the west.

John Lawler, superintendent of the Chicago, Milwaukee and St. Paul Railroad, supervised the building of rail lines from Beloit, Iowa, on the Sioux River south of Canton, South Dakota, to Sioux Falls. He also supervised the construction of the Milwaukee line that ran from Beloit,

The pastor and children of St. Brigid's Parish, Walshtown. Courtesy of Jean Hauger.

through Worthing, Lennox, Marion Junction, Scotland, Springfield, to Running Water.

The town of Tyndall developed to the north of the Bon Homme settlement. Bridget Cogan and Peter Byrne were among those Bon Homme residents who relocated to Tyndall, along the rail line. Bon Homme's chances of survival were further curtailed when the channel of the Missouri River moved nearly two miles to the south of the town as a result of the floods of the spring of 1881.

The Finley settlement in Turner County disappeared as Marion Junction developed at the point where the Milwaukee line from Sioux Falls was connected directly with the line running west from Beloit. [26] James Madden and Philip Devitt assisted in the construction of the Milwaukee through the Worthing and Lennox area. James Madden constructed a grain terminal along the line at Worthing.[3] The Milwaukee line was extended to Running Water in 1879. The settlement of Running Water grew to a population of

Father George Sheehan organized several Irish parishes, and was involved in the efforts to relocate orphaned, Irish children from the streets of Boston to Irish families in Dakota. Courtesy of the Archives of the Diocese of Sioux Falls.

nearly 1800 by the year 1880. The community included St. Stephen's Catholic Church. It also included seven saloons, a hotel, and three brothels. Plans were developed to build a bridge from Running Water to Niobrara. The bridge was never built. A river ferry was used in its place.[4] [16]

Michael O'Shea, the former trading post operator, was the first postmaster of the settlement. The James Malone, Patrick Martin, Francis and James Donnelly, William Dooley, Thomas McGoldrick, Hunt and Foley families made up the Irish Settlement. The Martins, Malones and Hunts arrived in 1873. A roundhouse for the train engines and a stockyards were built on the Malone property. Running Water remained an active community during the period that it was the terminus of the Milwaukee Road rail line.

The Sioux Falls settlement became an important commercial center due to the fact that it served as the junction of several rail lines. The railroad from the the Catholic Colonization colonies in southwestern Minnesota was extended to Sioux Falls in 1880. The Great Northern Railroad was extended through northwestern Iowa to Beloit and Sioux City in 1880. Mary McGivern McDermott assisted in the plotting of the towns of Alvord and Lester. Rock Valley is named for a region of Ireland.

Railroad workers near Sioux Falls. Irish laborers built many of the rail lines into and throughout Dakota Territory. Courtesy of Leonard Tripp.

The 1882-83 <u>Sioux Falls City Directory</u> lists Irish born railroad workers Philip Cannon, James and John Finley, John Gilmore, John Mallady, James Mceavy, Henry McMoran, F. McMann, James Sheehan, Charles and Bartley Smythe and John Welsh residing in the town. Irish born Ellen Smith and Barbara Welch were employed as servants. The importance of the Sioux Falls settlement was signified by the ordination of William Maher by Bishop John Spalding in Milwaukee in 1878. He was immediately sent to be the first resident Catholic pastor of Sioux Falls. Bishop Marty and Father Christian Knauf from the Catholic Colonization Bureau in Adrian, Minnesota had purchased the land for the construction of St. Michael's Church in the fall of 1879. It is difficult to speculate if Bishop John Ireland foresaw the day when the seat of the Dakota Vicariate would be moved to Sioux Falls from Yankton.

The area to the south and east of 8th Street and Phillips Avenue, the main corner of Sioux Falls, became the location of many Irish residences.[5] Michael Gerin, Peter Gilman, J.J. Boylan and Daniel Donahoe all established businesses located from Phillips Avenue at 8th Street, south to 13th Street and Second Avenue. The location of the St. Michael's church on the bluffs overlooking the valley changed the focus of the activities of the Irish community in Sioux Falls. The Irish became an important part of the commercial and social makeup of the Sioux Falls community.

The Wilcox Hotel, Running Water Irish Settlement, 1890. Courtesy of the South Dakota State Historical Society.

By 1886, Finton McMahon had established a Sioux Falls residence. He was employed in one of the town's many quarry operations. In 1886, Finton's sister, Mary, moved with her new husband, Joseph Kirby to live in Sioux Falls. After taking the Dakota Territory bar examination, Joseph was admitted to practice law in November, 1886. He began as an employee of the Bailey and Davis law firm. In 1888, he opened his own law practice. In 1900, Joseph Kirby began the Western Surety Company in Sioux Falls. Finton McMahon would eventually become a prize fight promoter.

In 1887, the East Sioux Falls and Rowena communities developed around quarries owned by J.E. Riley of Omaha and Thomas J. Ryan of Dubuque.[6] [62]

The Bloomingdale grist mill was constructed in 1868 by James McHenry and John W. Turner. Turner moved in 1875 to the settlement of Turner, near present day, Davis, South Dakota. [44] He established another grist mill that was flooded out in 1881. McHenry established a store at Bloomingdale and leased the mill

Michael Gerin's Livery and Store was located on Phillips Avenue in Sioux Falls. Michael Gerin is on the left. Courtesy of the Center for Western Studies.

out. Another mill was established at Lodi, by H. H. Ruud and John Fisher, John Turner's son-in-law. Fisher left the area in 1877.

After planning, but not completing, a Vermillion brewery in 1870, James McHenry, in 1872, acquired ownership of a steam mill. Beginning in 1873 and until 1877 the mill was operated by James G. Botsford.[7] After a brief journey to the Black Hills, Botsford moved to Sioux Falls. McHenry sold the mill in 1878. There is no record of what became of McHenry or his wife, Mary. The mill continued in operation. In 1878, the Missouri River main channel moved north. This allowed freight to be unloaded at Vermillion and transported to Ft. Pierre. John Dougherty became involved in this independent freighting business. Tons of Bloomingdale and Vermillion flour were shipped to the Black Hills.

In 1872, McHenry was, at the time, the president of the Irish Colonization Convention. Another representative from the convention was Thomas F. Sloan, who later became a faculty member at the University of South Dakota. Professor Sloan wrote a History of the Catholic Church in Vermillion, S.D., 1859-1899.

The Chicago, Milwaukee, and St. Paul Railroad constructed a rail line from Beloit, Iowa to Chamberlain. Irish settlers established

Joseph Kirby, lawyer and founder of the Western Surety Company. Courtesy of the Kirby family.

communities at Parker, Monroe, Dolton, Bridgewater, Emery, Alexandria, Spencer, Farmer, Mitchell, White Lake, Plankinton, Kimball, Pukwana and Chamberlain. [45-58] Father Meinrad McCarthy performed the first mass in Mitchell in the upstairs of a bar owned by Irish Catholic settlers. They used beer kegs to form a temporary altar.[8] The Kimball settlement began with the arrival in 1880 of Mike and Thomas Conley, Henry C. Smith, and John D. Lawler. Mike and Tom Carney, Dennis Brady, Tim Farrell, Jacob Rush, Bartholomew Ryan, "Irish" John Smith, John Walsh, the Gavins and Purcells arrived by 1884. [56]

Irish communities that were established at Hartford, Humboldt and Montrose continued along the railroad. [59-61] Several of settlers from the St. Michael's community established residences in Dell Rapids after the arrival of the railroad. Garretson's Irish residents arrived with the creation of the town on the Great Northern in 1889. [114]

Msgr. Thomas Flynn, Madison's Catholic pastor and pitcher. Later, the town umpire and Vicar General of the Catholic Diocese of Sioux Falls. Courtesy of the Diocese of Sioux Falls.

Irish settlements in Moody County were located at Egan, Flandreau, Colman, and St. Michael's. [63-65] Flandreau was a mission of the Catholic Colonization settlement at Avoca, Minnesota. In 1881 the competition for the construction of the Catholic Church developed between Flandreau and Egan. The August 11, 1881 *Flandreau Enterprise* noted,"While there are comparatively few Catholics residing in Flandreau, there are a large number in the country". The newspaper believed that the Flandreau town location would best serve the Catholic farmers, who were predominantly Irish. Irish born, John Brogan and Michael Quinlan would served as the first two resident pastors. Thomas Quick arrived in the early 1890s.

Lake County Irish communities were created at Badus, Ramona, and Madison. [66] The pastor of the St. Thomas Church in Madison was Father Thomas Flynn, a Milwaukee native, who arrived in 1880. Besides his duties as a local pastor, Father Flynn served as the Madison's baseball team's pitcher. He later served as the town's umpire. The athletic fields in Madison are named Flynn Field in his honor. At a time when many Protestant clergy believed that baseball was a sinful activity, the Irish American pastor of St. Thomas Parish in Madison was one of the leading pitchers in the area. Flynn served as the Vicar General of the Diocese of Sioux Falls.

Miner County Irish settlements were located at Carthage and Fedora. [67-68] Irish communities were located at the Sanborn County settlements of Artesian, Letcher, and Woonsocket. [69-71] Wessington Springs in Jerauld County had an Irish community. [115] Richard F. Lyons homesteaded in Lake County in 1878. In 1883, Lyons led a group of settlers from Burr Oak, Iowa to Lake County, near Madison.

The center of Irish settlement in Brookings County was at Elkton. [22] The Irish presence in Elkton was substantial from the beginning of the community. In 1898 there were 50 active members of the Ancient Order of the Hibernians in Elkton. Dr. William Dunn of Sioux Falls, a descendent of settlers from both the Greeley Colony in Nebraska, and the Elkton community has documented one hundred and seven different family surnames that can be traced to the Elkton settlement. Although the settlements were never organized along purely clan lines, the author has not found instances of whole clans or villages arriving enmass to settle, there are several instances of people moving from one area of Irish settlement to another. The Elkton settlement was established in 1878. The Irish people located in Parnell Township, Brookings, County, and Alton Township, to the southwest of Elkton. Many of the settlers came from the Caledonia settlement in Houston County, Minnesota. The population included twenty five Irish born settlers. The oldest settler was Irish born Cornelius O'Leary who arrived in Elkton in 1878 at the age of 104. He died in Elkton in 1888. Irish born Matthew Donahoe served as a Brookings County Commissioner from 1885 through 1888.

Edward Fitzgerald, who arrived in Emmet in 1870, would own 640 acres near Emmet, and two farms near Dell Rapids at the time of his death. Several of the people who became residents of the Northend Cathedral District of Sioux Falls arrived in the area as settlers at the various communities. They moved into the city during difficult times on the farms. Many Irish settlers became store owners in small, farm communities in Dakota.

Brookings and White also had Irish settlers. [73] The center of Irish settlement in Kingsbury County was at DeSmet. [74] The Irish settlers at DeSmet included: Patrick Caroll, Mike Fitzpatrick, Fred Reese, William and Edward Denevan, Mary and Thomas O'Connor, Charles Mathews,Thomas Matthews, Jerry and Michael Dailey, Martin Brislan, Frank Gillespie, Patrick and Thomas O'Hora, Luke Kelly and Thomas O'Hara. Thomas O'Reilly served as the Catholic pastor beginning in 1880. Irish settlers were also present at Arlington, Iroquois, and Oldham. [75-77]

The Irish settlements at both Huron and Cavour were quite extensive. [78-79] Irish born M. J. Dinneen arrived in Huron in 1880. Micheal Dineen established the Jim River House, which eventually became the Dakota House. The hotel became the early center of social and business activity. Catholic Church services were held in the hotel for three years. Dineen became an active real estate person during Huron's first years. J. W. Shannon established the

Huron Tribune in 1880. T. J. Nichol, Superintendent of the Dakota Division of the Chicago, Northwestern Railroad, donated land on which to build a Catholic church in Huron. Ed Murnaine and John Conlin assisted in the masonry work on the church. Settlers included: Richard Tobin, John McDonnell, John Fleming, John Hanley, Martin Issenhuth, Mike Morrissey, Joe Breen, Joe Malone, G. Leepe, John McMahon, Jerry Mcnerney, Sheldon Osborn and John Farrell.

St. Patrick's Church in Cavour began and remains as one of the most active, rural Catholic communities in the region. The rail line from Huron to Pierre included Irish settlements at Miller, Highmore, Harrold, and Pierre. [80-83]

Joseph Kirley had arrived at Ft. Randall in 1865, having worked on the riverboats from Montana. He moved to Yankton in 1866. He worked as a woodcutter at Big Cedar Island, thirty-five miles north of Ft. Randall in 1868. He also worked at the Lower Brule Agency as a clerk. Owners of the Agency store were Simon Eisman and Jack Kelly. The post commander was a Captain Daugherty. He then worked at the cattle camp operated by Bill Paxton and Jack Morrow, located fifteen miles north of Ft. Pierre. By 1872, the contract with the U. S. Government for the cattle was terminated. Joe Kirley had begun as the stage station keeper in 1870. He chose to remain at the camp, which came to be called Kirley's Landing. Joseph had also

Father Robert Haire, priest, author, and politician, helped establish the Columbia settlement. He served Irish Catholics throughout northeastern Dakota. Courtesy of the Archives of the Presentation Sisters.

married Alice Seemans of Bon Homme during this period. By 1878, Joseph and Alice had established a residence, called Mattoe, on the east bank of the Missouri River, opposite Ft. Pierre. In 1880, the Chicago and Northwestern Railroad chose to extend their line to the Mattoe site. The settlement of Pierre would soon develop upon the site of Mattoe.

In the glacial lake region of Dakota, directly west of the Catholic Colonization Bureau settlements of Minnesota, Irish settlements were established at Clear Lake, Estelline, Hazel, Naples, Raymond, Watertown, Waverly, Revillo, Milbank, Waubay, and Webster. [84-94] Father Timothy Ryan of the Colonization Bureau in Graceville, Minnesota served the people of the Clear Lake settlers.[9] Father John Flannigan established a Catholic parish at Webster in 1884.

Father Robert Emmet Haire led a group of Irish American Catholics from Michigan to the settlement of Columbia on the James River in 1880. Besides being the leader of the community of settlers at Columbia, Father Haire served as a circuit-riding priest throughout the central and eastern part of Dakota. [95]

Irish populations developed along the Chicago, Northwestern Railroad at Ashton, Athol, Turton, Conde, Verdon, Redfield and

P. H. O'Neill, "The Cattle King of Dakota", operated a cattle ranch near Faulkton, Dakota Territory. Courtesy of the Archives of the Diocese of Sioux Falls.

Groton. [97-103] Father Haire transferred his parish from Columbia to Aberdeen with the coming of the Great Northern Railroad. [96] Father Haire, who began his life as a Protestant, received land from Frank Hagerty, an Irish Protestant, to establish Sacred Heart parish in Aberdeen. Hagerty would later serve as an immigration official for the Territory of Dakota. Irish Americans settled in Ipswich and Mobridge on the Great Northern. [104-105] Pollock in western Campbell County had a smattering of Irish settlers. [116]

The Missouri Hills country was settled like much all of the ranch country of West River South Dakota. Onida, Orient and Lebenon all had Irish settlers. [106-108] The first settlers in Faulk County arrived in 1882. Faulkton became a station of the Chicago, Milwaukee, and St. Paul Railroad in 1886. [109] Settlers included the newspaper editor, H.A. Humphrey, Patrick Duggan, J.L. Grath, Nicholas Kennedy, and P.H. O'Neill. By 1900, O'Neill's cattle operation had 22,000 acres under fence. P. H. O'Neill, an Irish Catholic, was called the "Cattle King of South Dakota."

Wagner and Geddes in Charles Mix County had substantial Irish settlement at their inception. [110-111] Settlers in the Wagner area included Mike and Thomas Harney, Thomas McCabe, William Fitzgerald, William Lyons, John Delaney, J. E. Larkin, Andrew McKenna, William McKennan, John Burke, Ed Bradley, John Morgan, Thomas Cole, William Donahue, Pat Lyon and Pat Conner. This occurred at the time of the opening of the Yankton Reservation.

McHenry and Stutsman County in what is now North Dakota bear the names of two important, territorial political figures. The town of McHenry, which is currently located in northcentral North Dakota, was established in 1899. It was named for E.H. McHenry, chief engineer of the Jamestown & Northern Railroad.

John T. Duffy was a survivor of over a year in prison in England for his involvement in the Fenian uprising of 1867 in Ireland. In 1881, Duffy arrived in Grafton, Walsh County, Dakota Territory. He helped to establish the *Grafton Herald*. He entered politics where he served as an assistant register of deeds. He later became the secretary of the North Dakota Democratic Party State Central Committee.[10]

Duffy died at a time in the spring of 1914, when the Irish Nationalists were returning their fallen "Fenian" dead from exile for politically charged burials in Ireland. Jerimiah O'Donovan Rossa was on his deathbed in California at the time of Duffy's death. Duffy's family refused to allow his body to be returned for burial in Ireland. He was buried in North Dakota. Rossa died shortly after. His body was returned to Ireland. Padraig Pearse's famous funeral oration was given at Rossa's funeral.

At the time of the 1890 census, North Dakota recorded 8,174 residents who had been born in Ireland and England. Many of those were Irish.[11]

ANNA SWEENEY

A Prairie fire struck the plains of Dakota in April of 1881. The Sweeneys were recent homesteaders near Okobojo, Dakota Territory. Anna Sweeney was on her father's farm as the fire approached. During her attempts at trying to save the family's livestock she was caught up in the fire and burned to death. This ballad set to the hymn, "Come Thou Fount of Every Blessing" honors Anna's brief life.

On the wild Dakota Prairie
Where the sun is ever bright
Lived a fair and youthful maiden
Merry voice and footsteps light
Many friends were gathered around her,
Many lovers claimed her hand,
But the one that Anna favored
Dwelled within a distant land.

When in haste there comes a letter
Soon he'd come and claim his bride
To take her from the wild Dakotas
To his home in joy and pride.
Soon the bridal robe was ready
And the time was drawing near
When the heart of Anna Sweeney
Must be torn from friends so dear.

Do not leave me said her father
For my locks are turning grey
And my heart would break without you
One more summer with me stay
Thus he pleaded night and morning
She at last the promise gave
For she knew her aged father
Fast was hastening to the grave.

On the morn of April second
Long to be remembered day
Anna's father left their dwelling
For the village miles away
Little dreamed he of the sorrow
That was lurking in his path
Saw he not the fiery fiend
Rushing on in quenchless wrath.

Anna in their humble dwelling
5aw the hungry flames draw nigh
From the stall she loose the cattle
Then for safety tried to fly
One more moment she would of reached it
But the hungry flames drew nigh
Clasp her only for a moment
Leaves her lifeless and are gone.

Oh! that day of bitter sorrow
Oh! that day of fear and fright
Who so happy in the morning
Lay in ashes long ere night
In the village Anna's father
Chats with friends in joy and mirth
Telling them of Anna's promise
And his daughter's priceless word.

When in haste there comes a message
Told with quick and startled breath
Of the quick and dire destruction
And of Anna's painful death
See the old man reel and stagger
See his look of deep despair
Pity him the aged father
With his locks of silvery hair.

It will kill him said the neighbors
For he has lost his joy and pride
It was true ere summer ended
He was laid by Anna's side
I have told this as I heard it
From the friends who knew them best
Truth is stranger still than fiction
Life is sad but sweet is rest.

1   Walshtown File, Diocese of Sioux Falls Archives.

2   George Kingsbury, <u>Compendium of Biography, Kingsbury's History of South Dakota</u>, (Pierre, South Dakota, 1915), S. J. Clarke Co., Chicago, Page 156.

3   Conversations with Marian Devitt, 1976-1990. <u>Worthing Centennial History</u>, Worthing, South Dakota, 1972.

4   Mary Lou Livingston, <u>History of Running Water</u>, Yankton, South Dakota, 1989.

5   Perkins Bros, <u>History of Southeastern Dakota</u>, Sioux City, Iowa, 1880.

6   Robert Kolbe, editor, "Rowena", <u>History of Minnehaha County</u>, Sioux Falls, 1989.

7   Dr. Herbert Schell, <u>History of Clay County</u>, (Clay County Historical Society, Vermillion, South Dakota, 1985), Pages 10-12, 17-35, 54, 140, 174.

8   Mitchell File, parish records, Diocese of Sioux Falls Archives.

9   Humphrey Monihan, "Archbishop Ireland's Colonies", <u>Acta Et Dicta</u>, Archdiocese of St. Paul, St. Paul, Minnesota, 1934.

10   <u>Walsh County Heritage, A Story of Walsh County and Its Pioneers</u>, Walsh County Historical Society, Page 118.

11   Elwyn Robinson, <u>History of North Dakota</u>, University of Nebraska Press, Lincoln, 1966), Page 146.

CHAPTER 8

THE IRISH CONTRIBUTION TO
THE POLITICS OF DAKOTA
AND THE IRISH NATION

John Sweetman was present at the beginning of the The National Land League, whose principles would influence Irish politics for the next four decades. Sweetman also nominated Charles Parnell for the presidency of the League.[1] Parnell would dominate Irish politics during the decade of the 1880s. Rejecting the beliefs of the Fenians that Ireland would obtain its freedom through armed revolt, the Land Leaguers believed that Irish independence could be obtained through involvement in the English parliamentary system. Parnell, a Protestant, through his presence in the English Parliament, attempted to carry out a series of land reforms in Ireland. The Irish believed that the true owners of the land of Ireland were the peasants, the people displaced by the seizure of the land by the English over the previous two hundred years. The system of land ownership in Ireland was to be removed and the land returned to the Irish peasant as a functional, political entity. The peasants would reap the land's harvest as they had done for centuries prior to English occupation and the imposition of the land ownership system.

The financial support for the political activities of the Land League came, for a large part, from the contributions of the Irish in America. Charles Parnell visited America in 1879, prior to the formal organization of the Land League. Included in the series of speeches and meetings were visits to Des Moines and Chicago.[2]

The Irish National League of America was organized as the formal political body in Canada and the United States. Patrick Egan, who had immigrated from Ireland to Nebraska through the support of John Fitzgerald, became the president. He served as the leading fundraiser and Charles Parnell's representative in America. The executive office of the National Land League was located in Lincoln, Nebraska, Fitzgerald's place of residence. J.P. Sutton, the

League's secretary, also resided in Lincoln. He became involved in the Land League in Quebec, Canada and eventually moved to Nebraska.[3]

John Brennan, by this time the well established editor of the Sioux City Journal, and a polished public speaker, was involved in the Land League's activities. Brennan gave speeches throughout the country. At various times he shared the podium with either Charles Parnell or Patrick Egan. Brennan began his involvement in American politics as a Democrat.

Realizing that the Republican Party was the dominant, major party of the the decade, many Irish politicians became involved in Republican politics in hopes of improving the lot of the Irish national movement by influencing the policies of the American government. John Brennan was one of these Irish Americans. Brennan spoke at political rallies for Republican presidential candidate, James Blaine, in both the 1884 and 1888 presidential elections. He turned down an ambassadorship in South America because of the poor health of his wife and his job responsibilities in Sioux City.[4]

Thomas Burns arrived in Mitchell, South Dakota, in 1883. He immediately became involved in local politics. He served as the U.S. Government Land Agent for Davison County.

Richard F. Lyons served as the Lake County delegate to the Dakota State Constitutional Convention in July of 1889. He later moved to Vermillion, where he served as the state chairman to the Democratic Party from 1908-1912. He served as mayor of Vermillion from 1916-1918.

Charles H. Burke homesteaded in Beadle County, Dakota, in 1882. The following year, he moved to Hughes County, where he was admitted to the state bar in 1886. He was elected as a Republican to the U.S. House of Representatives in 1898.[5] He served in the House from 1899 through 1906. He was reelected in 1908 and served until 1912. In 1912 he was defeated in the election for U.S. Senator. His most noteworthy piece of legislation during his congressional career was the Burke Act. The Burke Act gave the Department of the Interior discretionary power to issue a patent in fee simple whenever they deemed a Native American allottee competent to manage his own affairs. In 1921, former congressman Burke was appointed the United States Commissioner of Indian Affairs. He served in the position until May of 1929.[6]

Daniel Murphy was forced to leave Ireland due to his activities in Ireland in support of the Land League reforms. Murphy located in the Aberdeen, Dakota area as an employee of the Chicago, Milwaukee, and St. Paul Railroad. His sons, Jerry and John became lawyers representing the Milwaukee Railroad and John Morrell and Company respectfully. Jerimiah Murphy, currently an influential political figure in South Dakota, is the grandson of Daniel Murphy.[7] Longtime South Dakota Republican leader, Joseph Barnett, was a descendant of George Barnett, who moved from the Catholic Colonization Bureau settlement at Adrian, Minnesota to Sioux Falls in 1878. Sioux Falls resident Daniel Donahoe's sons, Den and Stephen, became involved in Democratic politics. Stephen ran for the U.S. Senate against R.F. Pettigrew.[8] Den served as the Minnehaha County Sheriff.

George Walsh became involved in Democratic politics while a resident of the Aberdeen area in the 1880's. Walsh eventually

Den Donahoe, son of Daniel (O'Donaghue) Donahoe, served as the Minnehaha County, South Dakota Sheriff. Courtesy of Patty Donahoe Fokken.

located in Montana, where he was elected to the United States Senate.

It is rather ironic that Irish settlers of Dakota would involve themselves in the homestead experience and the establishment of a landholding system based on the British system. The result being the subsequent dissolution of the Native American tribes of the region's landbase and tribal, clan based, society. At the same time, they paid lip service and made financial contributions to the Fenian and Land League activities. Tenets of both Irish National organizations emphasized the end of English control of the land of Ireland and the return of Ireland's land to its original owners.

Father Robert Haire began the *Dakota Catholic American*, the official publication of the Vicariate of Dakota in Aberdeen in 1887. The only available copy of the publication is its initial issue. The contents of the first issue include discussions of church issues and activities, and features on the establishment of church and missions in the Dakota Territory. There are no discussions of current political issues. Although further complete documentation of the paper's contents are not available, subsequent issues involved statements by Father Haire that supported the views of the farm protest movement. As a result, editorship of the paper was taken from Haire by Bishop Martin Marty.

The *Dakota Catholic* appeared in February of 1889. Its first editor was Father Thomas Hopkins, an Irish American and Bishop Marty's secretary. It was published in Sioux City. *The Northwestern Chronicle*, an Irish American newspaper edited by John Brennan, also began publication in Sioux City at this time.

The contents of the *Dakota Catholic* included summaries of the political events occurring in Ireland and among Irish Americans, and poetry extolling the Catholic Church's resistance to "The evil day of England's sin". The May 18, 1889, issue features Father Hopkins' "Priest's Visit to Ft. Randall". Father Hopkins viewed the Fort Randall community as an ideal example of a Catholic community. Ft. Randall would close in 1892.

The July 6, 1889, issue included the editorial condemnation of secret societies, including the Clan An Gael. The July 13 issue featured an editorial condemning people's misconceptions tying the terrorist activities of the Clan An Gael to the political activities of the American National League. The August 3 issue featured an article on Father Christian Knauf and the dedication of a new church building at the Catholic Colonization Colony at Adrian, Minnesota.The August 10, 1889, issue featured a letter from Father George Sheehan who was back visiting his brother, the Catholic Bishop of Waterford, Ireland. The emphasis on the politics of Ireland in the official publication of the Catholic Church in Dakota reflected Father Hopkins' perception that the Irish were the majority, Catholic, ethnic group in Dakota at the time of statehood in 1889.

The author cannot help but recall Monsignor Leonard Sullivan, an excellent South Dakota and Catholic historian, first telling about Father Robert Haire. He emphasized that Father Haire believed that the strength of the Catholic Church in Dakota was to be found in the small, rural, farm based communities, and not the large city congregations. The beliefs of the first Irish Catholic settlers of Dakota, with whom Haire was involved, must have influenced Haire and other Populist era political leaders. Belief in the need to protect the operations of the family farm from outside political and economic interests.

Statements by Bishop Paul Dudley in 1989, include his belief that the strength of the Catholic Church in South Dakota lies in the small, rural congregations. A belief first developed by the Irish during the Territorial period of Dakota.

1   John Sweetman, "The Sweetman Catholic Colony of Currie, Minnesota, A Memoir", <u>Acta Et Dicta, Volume 3</u>, (Archdiocese of St. Paul, St. Paul, Minnesota, 1911), Page 41

2   Homer Calkins, "The Irish In Iowa", <u>The Palimpsest</u>, Volume XVV, No. 2, February, 1964 (Iowa State Historical Society, Iowa City, Iowa, 1964), Page 78.

3   *Daily State Journal,* Lincoln, Nebraska), June 22, 1886, Page 5, Column 3.

4   A. F. Allen, <u>History of Sioux City Newspapers</u>, (Sioux City, Iowa, 1925), Pages 41-43.

5   O. W. Coursey, <u>Who's Who In South Dakota,</u> (Mitchell, South Dakota, 1913, Page 47.

6   Dr. Herbert Schell, <u>History of South Dakota</u>, (Lincoln, Nebraska, 1968), Pages 261, 262, 335, 338.

7   Jerimiah Murphy, Conversation, May, 1989, Sioux Falls, South Dakota.

8   Robert Karolevitz, <u>Martin Marty, the Black Robe Lean Chief,</u> (Yankton, South Dakota, 1978), Pages 120-121.

CHAPTER 9

THE IRISH POPULATION AT THE ARRIVAL OF STATEHOOD, 1889

Father Thomas Hopkins, in the *Dakota Catholic* of the fall of 1889, would estimate the Catholic population of Dakota to be approximately 48,000 people out of a total population of 325,000. The Irish population was estimated at 22,000. He believed that the Irish people made up the largest ethnic group among the Catholics. Interestingly, he stated that he had spent the past months traveling the territory. He commented that he saw train load after train load of new arrivals. He observed that most of them were Germans.

Within in a few years, the German Catholics would become the largest ethnic group among the Catholics of the state of South Dakota. The population as a whole would reflect the fact that the Germans had become the largest ethnic group among the immigrants in Dakota. The Irish would become a significant ethnic group among the over twenty ethnic groups which settled in Dakota.

The Irish were one of many groups which settled in the region attempting to preserve their cultural and spiritual heritage. A distinct Irish of Dakota ethnic identity began to develop during the territorial experience. This was not just a negative reaction to discrimination and bias from outside the Irish communities but a positive attempt at using Irish perseverance, humor, and patience to endure the climate and strange characters the Irish immigrants encountered. Much as the Irish had absorbed invaders over the many centuries, the Irish of Dakota would patiently await the changes in language and lifestyles occurring among the other ethnic groups of Dakota.

The Irish population would include miners in the Black Hills. The largest population center in early South Dakota was in the Lead, Deadwood and Central City region. This study has documented a large Irish American presence in these mining camps. The Irish of Dakota, like Irishmen throughout America in the late 19th Century, carried out the most strenuous and dangerous work in order to put food on the table. Military life was not considered the most glamorous of occupations in the 19th Century.

The Irish were also farmers, returning to the land in order to preserve their true spiritual heritage. Some settlers were Irish born. Many were the second and younger sons of Irish immigrants from the Famine years of 1845-48. The oldest son inherited the farm in Wisconsin, Illinois, Minnesota or Iowa. The younger sons moved west to Dakota. The younger sons of Irish families in the period from 1890 to 1910 would seek land in West River Dakota. Many had come to Eastern Dakota during the territorial period.

Ireland, until the massive population explosion of the late eighteenth and early nineteenth century, had been a remote, but beautiful land. The lifestyle was quite rural. Both the beauty and the remoteness were found once again by the Irish settlers to the region. Celtic life had included extensive cattle raising. Irish men tended to wait until their late thirties to marry. The cowboy lifestyle of West River Dakota would include both of these elements.

Control of the household by Irish women, both in social and economic terms, a traditional practice in Ireland, was re-established within the farming and rural communities of Dakota. The tradition

Bridget Cogan later established a residence in Tyndall, Dakota Territory. Bridget is seated in the carriage. Courtesy of Joan Wall.

of educating Irish women as a means of retaining their economic and social position was established. The extended Irish family, with the mother as the dominant character, was continued after settlement in Dakota.

The popularity of baseball, America's pastime, was spread across the country in the years after the Civil War by Irish American veterans. Baseball was one aspect of the "sporting" life of the American male of the late 19th Century. It also included frequenting of saloons, the playing of dance and party music, horse racing, and participation in various social endeavors such as the Ancient Order of the Hibernians. Irish Nationalists of the late 19th Century expressed renewed interest in the traditional Celtic sport of hurling, and in loyalty to your community's Irish football team as an expression of their nationalism. Irish in America attempted to popularize these sports in America. After little success in this endeavor the Irish population took to the supporting and playing of

(Left to right) Marie Madden Devitt (the author's great grandmother), Ed Devitt (his great uncle), Philip Aylward (his grandfather), Marian Devitt (his predecessor as the family historian), and Kate Devitt Aylward (his grandmother). Courtesy of Peggy Aylward Kemp.

baseball as an expression of their patriotic spirit. These activities were contributed to the new experience of Dakota Territory in a large part by the Irish American population.

The majority of the Irish people who arrived in Dakota during the territorial period were either Gaelic and English speaking, or English speaking people. They had been English speaking and not Gaelic speaking for only a generation or two. Survival in the years after the British occupation required the Irish to become English speaking. The Great Famine intensified the learning of English as a means of survival. In Dakota Territory, the majority of the English speaking people were either old stock Americans or first or second generation English speaking, Irish and Scottish people. Their language was more than likely a distinct form of Irish or Scots English. Many of the school teachers were Irish American women, like the author's grandmother, Kate Devitt Aylward. It is safe to say that the great many of the school teachers in Dakota, whose main job was to teach the immigrant population English, were Irish English speakers. None of the author's family, as one example, have ever been accused of speaking proper English. A careful linguistics

The children of Central City. The future of the Irish experience in Dakota Territory. Courtesy of the South Dakota Historical Society.

examination of the origins of the dialect of English spoken in both East River and West River Dakota should be carried out. The author has encountered various phrases that reflect continual usage in Dakota of Gaelic Irish syntax.

John Sweetman returned to Ireland after his failed colonization attempts of the 1880s. In 1911, he published a memoir of his experiences in the <u>Acta Et Dicta</u>, which was an official publication of the Catholic Archdiocese of St. Paul. He stated that, in his case, although helping Irish to settle on land in America was a failure, he did succeed in helping to establish a Catholic presence on the prairie.

Irish settlement in Dakota, with its origins that included involvement in extensive Fenian activities, was unique in many ways to related Irish settlement in the upper Midwest. Interest in and attempts at contributing to the struggle for Irish freedom continued among the Irish of the region. By 1890, people were doing so as Irish Americans and not as exiled Irishmen.

This study offered many facts and observations about this experience. The question whether settlement in Dakota resulted in the preservation in the true spirituality of the Celtic Irish people remains unresolved. Yes, the Irish did play a major role in the settlement of Dakota.

(Left) Tommy Walsh of the Walshtown community in Yankton County. Courtesy of Bill Walsh.

INDEX

BIBLIOGRAPHY

Manuscripts:

Cullen, Brother Franklin, C.S.C., Holy Cross in the Black Hills, The Dakota Apostolate, 1878-1897, Brothers of the Holy Cross, Mountain View, California, 1986. Manuscript at Diocese of Rapid City Archives, Rapid City.

Droda, Richard, Irish Colonization In Nebraska, O'Neill and Greeley, Racial Elements in State, W.P.A. Project, Lincoln, Nebraska, 1936. Manuscript at Nebraska State Historical Society, Lincoln, Nebraska.

Duratschek, Sister Claudia, O.S.B., The Beginning of Catholicism in South Dakota, Dissertation, Catholic University of America, Catholic University Press, Yankton, South Dakota, Washington, D.C., 1943. Manuscript at Catholic Diocese of Rapid City Archives.

Egan, John, Catherine's Confession, Sioux Falls, 1988. Manuscript at Center for Western Studies, Augustana College, Sioux Falls.

Henthorne, Sister Mary E., The Irish Catholic Colonization Association of the United States, 1932. Manuscript at Nebraska State Historical Society, Lincoln, Nebraska.

Langen, Sister Mary Martin, O.P., General John O'Neill, Soldier, and Leader of Irish Colonization in America, University of Notre Dame, 1937, Manuscript at Nebraska State Historical Society, Lincoln, Nebraska.

Treacey, Sister DeSales P.B.V.M., "White Gold", Presentation Sisters in South Dakota. Manuscript in Diocese of Sioux Falls Archives and Presentation Heights Archives, Aberdeen.

Unknown author, Historical Sketch of St. Ambrose Parish since 1877, 1899. Church history, Deadwood file, Diocese of Rapid City Archives, Rapid City.

Public Documents:

F. & J. River and George A. Bailey, HR 1663, Forty First Congress, Second Session, March 31, 1870. The Congressional Globe containing th Debates and Proceedings of the Second Session, Forty First Congress, City of Washington, Office of the Congressional

Globe, City of Washington, 1870.

Land Records, Brule County Register of Deeds, Chamberlain, South Dakota.

Land Records, Minnehaha County Register of Deeds, Sioux Falls, South Dakota.

Military Records, National Archives, Denver Branch, Building 48, Denver Federal Center, Denver, Colorado.

Books:

Allen, A. F., History of Sioux City Newspapers, Sioux City, Iowa, 1925.

Athearn, Robert G., Thomas Francis Meagher: An Irish Revolutionary in America, University of Colorado Studies Series in History, No. 1.   University of Colorado Press, Boulder, Colorado, 1959.

Bailey, Dana, History of Minnehaha County, Sioux Falls, South Dakota, 1899.

Brown, Thomas N., Irish - American Nationalism, 1870 - 1890, J. B. Lippicott Co., 1966.

Calkin, Homer, The Palimpsest, "The Irish In Iowa", Published monthly by the State Historical Society of Iowa, Iowa City, Iowa, February, 1964.

Cash, Dr. Joseph, Mining the Homestake, University of Iowa Press, Iowa City, Iowa.

Casper, Henry, S. J., History of the Catholic Church in Nebraska, Volume 1, Bruce Press, Milwaukee, 1960.

Catholic Colonization Bureau, Guide to an Unsurpassed Farming Region in Southern Minnesota and Eastern Dakota, St. Paul, Minnesota, 1879.

Catholic Directories, Dioceses of St. Paul and Omaha, 1878, 1879, 1880, 1881, Sadlier & Co., New York.

A Century of History of Silver City, 1876 - 1976, Silver City, South Dakota, 1976.

Collins, Charles, Collins' History and Directory of the Black Hills, 1878 - 1879, Sioux City, 1879.

Duffy, Mary Consuela, S.B.S., Katherine Drexel, Sisters of Blessed

Sacrament Guild, Philadelphia, Pennsylvania, 1966, 1972.

Ellis, Peter Beresford, The Rising of the Moon, St. Martin's Press, New York, 1987.

Funchion, Michael, editor, Irish American Voluntary Organizations, Greenwood Press, Westport, Connecticut, 1983.

Gibson, Dale, Gisbon, Lee and Harvey,Cameron, Enos Stutsman, Attorney for the Frontier, University of Manitoba Press, Winnipeg, 1983.

Hagerty, Frank H., A Dictionary of Dakota Conveniently Arranging A Multitude of Facts About the Resources and Capabilities of the Great Territory Soon to Become Two States, Aberdeen, 1889.

Hale, William Harlan, Horace Greeley, Voice of the People, New York, 1947.

History of the Counties of Woodbury and Plymouth, Iowa, A Warner and Co. Publishers, Sioux City, Iowa, 1891.

The History of Dubuque County, Iowa, A History of the County, its Center, Town, etc. Chicago Western Historical Company, 1880.

History of the St. Peter and Paul Parish, Flandreau, Flandreau, South Dakota.

Jones, Peter and Nolli, Melvin G., editors, Ethnic Chicago, William B. Erdmans Publishing Company, Grand Rapids, Michigan, 1981.

Karolevitz, Robert F., Martin Marty, the Black Robe Lean Chief, Yankton, South Dakota, 1978.

Karolevitz, Robert F., Yankton, A Pioneer Past, North Plain Press, Aberdeen, South Dakota, 1972.

Kingsbury, George, Compendium of Biographies: South Dakota, 1898, Chicago, Illinois, 1915.

Kruger, Marian, 1877 -1977, The 100th Birthday Anniversary of Saint Adrian's Catholic Church, Adrian, Minnesota, 1977.

Leen, J. P., History of St. Joseph's Church, Emmet, Emmet, South Dakota, 1946.

Livingston, Mary Lou, History of Running Water, Yankton, South Dakota, 1989.

Manahan, James, Trials of a Lawyer, An Autobiography, St. Paul, Minnesota, 1933.

Mattson, Gerald, Church On the Seven Mile Prairie, St. Joseph

Parish, Farmington, Minnesota, Farmington, Minnesota, 1982.

McClintock, J. S., Pioneer Days in the Black Hills, Deadwood, South Dakota, 1937.

Mooney, T. M., editor, The Fenian Movement, Mercier Press, Dublin and Cork, 1968, 1978.

McCrum, Robert, Cran, William, and MacNeil Robert, The Story of English, Penguin Books, New York, 1986.

Nolan, Hugh, editor, Pastoral Letters of the American Hierarchy, 1792 - 1970, Our Sunday Visitor, Inc. Huntington, Indiana, 1971.

O'Grady, Standish, History of Ireland, Volume 1, 2, Lemma Publishing Corporation, New York, 1878, 1970.

Passewitz, Gregory R., History of Greeley County, O'Neill, Nebraska.

Perkins Bros., History of Southeastern Dakota, Sioux City, Iowa, 1880.

Peterson, Susan and Vaughn-Robeson, Courtney, Women with Vision: The Presentation Sisters of South Dakota, 1880 - 1985, University of Illnois Press, Urbana, Chicago, London, 1988.

Peterson, E. Frank, Peterson's Illustrated Atlas of South Dakota, Vermillion, 1904.

Robinson, Elwyn, History of North Dakota, U. of Nebraska Press, Lincoln, Nebraska, 1966.

Rosen, Father Peter, Pa-Sa-Pa or the Black Hills of South Dakota, (St. Louis, Missouri, 1895).

Schell, Herbert, History of Clay County, Clay County Historical Society, Vermillion, South Dakota, 1985.

Shannon, James P., Catholic Colonization On The Western Frontier, University of Minnesota Press, Minneapolis, 1957.

Spalding, J. L., The Religious Mission of the Irish People and Catholic Colonization, The Catholic Publication Society, New York, 1880.

Spence, Clark, Territorial Politics in Montana, 1864 - 1889, University of Illnois Press, Urbana, Chicago, London, 1975.

Sullivan, T. D., A. M., and D. B., introduction and biographical notes, Speeches From the Dock, Dublin, revised edition, 1968.

Sweeney, David Francis, O.F.M., The Life of John Lancaster

Spalding, New York, 1965.
Tallent, Annie, The Black Hills Or the Last Hunting Grounds of the
Dakotahs, Centennial Edition, 1876-1976. Brevet Press, Sioux Falls,
1974.
Walker, Mabel Gregory, The Fenian Movement, Ralph Myles
Publisher Inc., Colorado Springs, Colorado, 1969.
Walsh County Historical Society, Walsh Heritage, A Story of Walsh
County And Its Pioneers, Walsh County, North Dakota.
Wittke, Carl, Irish in America, Louisiana State Press, Baton Rouge,
1956.

Articles:
Bennett, Richard, "Mormon Renegade: James Emmett at the
Vermillion, 1846", South Dakota History, Volume 15, No. 3, 1985,
South Dakota State Historical Society, Pierre.
DeJong, Gerald F., Dakota Resources: "A Preliminary Guide for
Studying Ethnic Groups in South Dakota, A Bibliographical Essay
", South Dakota History, Vol. 15, No. 1, 1985, South Dakota State
Historical Society, Pierre.
Fox, Lawrence, "The Case of the United States vs. William Barry",
South Dakota Historical Collections, 1943.
Gnirk, Adeline, " Wheeler the Cradle of Charles Mix County",
History of Charles Mix County, Burke, South Dakota, 1986.
Hall, Dr. Philip S., "The Promoters' Trail", Parts 1 - 4,, Dakota
Heritage Magazine, Fort Pierre, South Dakota, 1971.
Karolevitz, Bob, "An Irish Toast to Charley Collins", South Dakota
Magazine, March, 1986, Yankton, South Dakota.
Moynihan, Humphrey, "Archbishop Ireland's Colonies", Acta Et
Dicta, Archdiocese of St. Paul, St. Paul, Minnesota, 1934.
Robinson, Doane, "Fenians in South Dakota", Directory of South
Dakota, South Dakota State Historical Society, Pierre, South
Dakota, 1925.
Robinson, Doane, "Fenians In Dakota", South Dakota Historical
Collections, South Dakota Historical Society, Pierre, South Dakota,
1912.

Sweetman, John, "The Sweetman Catholic Colony of Currie, Minnesota, A Memoir", <u>Acta Et Dicta, Volume 3</u>, (1911), Archdiocese of St. Paul, St. Paul, Minnesota.

"Former Prelates of the Omaha See", *The True Voice*, Archdiocese of Omaha, June 11, 1959, Omaha, Nebraska.

Newspapers:

Dakota Catholic, Volume 1, No. 2 - No. 23, March 9, 1889 - August 10, 1889.